COOS COOPERATIVE

DISCARD

3 2881 00700456 7

641.5 BES
The best of Mr. Food. Volume
2 / [quick and easy recipes]

D1120216

DISCARD COOS BAY PUBLIC LIBRARY
COOS BAY OREGON

The Best of Mr. Food®

Volume 2

"If you're hungry for good food, try my tasty, timesavin' recipes in my newest cookbook collection. OOH IT'S SO GOOD!!®"

Pasta with Tomatoes,
Brie, and Basil, page 59

Fruited Acorn Squash,
page 103

Streusel Shortcake, page 166

The Best of Mr. Food®
Volume 2

Oxmoor
House®

©2001 by Oxmoor House, Inc.
Book Division of Southern Progress Corporation
P.O. Box 2463, Birmingham, Alabama 35201

All rights reserved. No part of this publication may be reproduced in any form or by any means without the prior written permission of the publisher, excepting brief quotes in connection with reviews written specifically for inclusion in a magazine or newspaper.

ISBN: 0-8487-2464-X
ISSN: 1534-5505

Printed in the United States of America
First Printing 2001

Mr. Food®, the Caricature Logo, and OOH IT'S SO GOOD!! are registered marks owned by Ginsburg Enterprises Incorporated.

Ginsburg Enterprises Incorporated
    Chief Executive Officer: Art Ginsburg
    Chief Operating Officer: Steven Ginsburg
    Vice President, Publishing: Caryl Ginsburg Fantel
    Vice President, Creative Business Development: Howard Rosenthal
    Vice President, Sales and Licensing: Thomas R. Palombo
    Director of Finance and Administration: Chester Rosenbaum

Oxmoor House, Inc.
    Editor-in-Chief: Nancy Fitzpatrick Wyatt
    Senior Foods Editor: Susan Carlisle Payne
    Senior Editor, Copy and Homes: Olivia Kindig Wells
    Art Director: James Boone

THE BEST OF MR. FOOD®, featuring the recipes of Mr. Food, Art Ginsburg
    Editor: Kelly Hooper Troiano
    Copy Editor: Donna Baldone
    Associate Art Director: Cynthia R. Cooper
    Designer: Kelly Davis
    Editorial Assistant: Jane E. Lorberau
    Publishing Systems Administrator: Rick Tucker
    Director, Test Kitchens: Elizabeth Tyler Luckett
    Assistant Director, Test Kitchens: Julie Christopher
    Recipe Editor: Gayle Hays Sadler
    Test Kitchens Staff: Jennifer A. Cofield,
       Gretchen Feldtman, R.D., David Gallent,
       Ana Price Kelly, Jan A. Smith
    Senior Photographer: Jim Bathie
    Photographer: Brit Huckabay
    Senior Photo Stylist: Kay E. Clarke
    Photo Stylist: Virginia R. Cravens
    Director, Production and Distribution: Phillip Lee
    Associate Production Manager: Theresa L. Beste
    Production Assistant: Faye Porter Bonner

Contributors:
Indexer: Mary Ann Laurens
Test Kitchens: Kathleen Royal Phillips, Kate M. Wheeler, R.D.

Cover: *Flourless Chocolate Torte, page 169*

WE'RE HERE FOR YOU!
We at Oxmoor House are dedicated to serving you with reliable information that expands your imagination and enriches your life. We welcome your comments and suggestions. Please write to us at:
    Oxmoor House, Inc.
    Editor, Best of Mr. Food,
    Volume 2
    2100 Lakeshore Drive
    Birmingham, AL 35209

To order additional publications, call 1-205-445-6560.

For more books to enrich your life, visit oxmoorhouse.com

Contents

Party Hearty 9

Fancy Schmancy Dinners 31

Easy Weeknight Suppers 61

Super Sideshow 89

Soup and Salad Bar 113

Breadshoppe Bounty 133

Sweet Inspiration 153

Cookie Jar Jubilee 183

Index 205

Welcome!!

"In my latest cookbook, you'll discover family-lovin' comfort food that has gotten easier, faster, and more delicious! Instead of spending hours in the kitchen, you can now spend more time with the gang savoring the flavors of these quick and easy recipes! To fit today's busy lifestyle, we've provided recipes with easy-to-find ingredients, numbered cooking steps that are oh-so-easy to follow, and great cooking and convenience tips throughout. In just minutes, you'll have mouthwatering appetizers, entrées, breads, sides, and desserts. This crowd-pleasin' book will have the gang coming back for more! OOH IT'S SO GOOD!!"

Mr. Food

Party Hearty

"These crowd-pleasin' appetizers and beverages make any time party time! See for yourself!"

Jalapeño Guacamole

4 cups

1	tomato, chopped

3	ripe avocados, peeled and mashed
¼	cup chopped onion
1	jalapeño pepper, chopped
1	tablespoon lemon juice
1	teaspoon salt

1 Reserve 1 tablespoon chopped tomato for garnish.

2 Place remaining chopped tomato in a medium bowl. Add avocado and remaining 4 ingredients; stir well. Sprinkle with reserved tomato. Serve with tortilla chips.

" I recommend seeding the fresh jalapeño pepper before chopping it if you'd like to cut down on the fiery flavor of this guacamole. If you can take the heat, add the pepper—seeds and all!"

10

Meaty Cheesy Dip

6 cups

1 pound ground chuck
½ pound ground hot pork sausage

1 (2-pound) loaf process cheese spread, cubed
1 (8-ounce) jar medium salsa

1 Brown ground chuck and sausage in a large skillet, stirring until meat crumbles; drain in a colander, discarding drippings.

2 Add cheese and salsa; cook over low heat, stirring constantly, until cheese melts. Serve with large corn chips.

Kick It Up!
If you want to turn up the heat a notch or two, substitute a 2-pound loaf of Mexican process cheese for regular. If that's still not enough, go for hot salsa. That'll do it!

Pizzeria Dip

16 appetizer servings

1   (8-ounce) package cream cheese, softened
1   (14-ounce) jar pizza sauce
½   cup chopped green bell pepper
½   cup chopped onion
2   cups (8 ounces) shredded mozzarella cheese
1   (2¼-ounce) can sliced ripe olives, drained

1 Spread cream cheese in bottom of a 9" pie plate; spread pizza sauce over cream cheese. Sprinkle green pepper and onion over pizza sauce. Sprinkle mozzarella cheese and olives evenly over vegetable mixture.

2 Microwave at HIGH 7 to 8 minutes, giving dish a half-turn at 2-minute intervals. Serve with tortilla chips or assorted crackers.

❝ When you need a snack in a snap, layer these few ingredients, and then buzz them in the microwave. You'll be greeted with a cheesy surprise as you dip into the melted mozzarella layer. Yum! ❞

Cranberry-Pecan Goat Cheese

8 to 10 appetizer servings

½ cup finely chopped dried cranberries
¼ cup finely chopped pecans
¼ teaspoon salt
1 (11-ounce) log goat cheese

1 Combine first 3 ingredients. Roll goat cheese in cranberry mixture, pressing firmly.

2 Wrap cheese log in plastic wrap, and chill. Serve with assorted crackers.

" The gang will think fancy schmancy when they dig into this elegant appetizer—and all you did was dress up a log of goat cheese! It's a grand starter to a festive holiday evening, and it's so-o-o easy!"

Fast 'n' Fabulous Fondue

1½ cups

⅔ cup half-and-half
1 teaspoon Worcestershire sauce
¾ teaspoon dry mustard
½ clove garlic, minced

2 cups (8 ounces) shredded sharp
    Cheddar cheese
1 tablespoon all-purpose flour

1 Combine first 4 ingredients in a medium saucepan. Cook over low heat, stirring often, until thoroughly heated (do not boil).

2 Combine cheese and flour, tossing well. Add cheese mixture to saucepan; stir until cheese melts.

3 Pour cheese mixture into a fondue pot or chafing dish. Serve warm with cubed French or Italian bread for dipping.

" Everything old is new again—and this classic party fixture from the '70s is no exception. I like to serve it with big chunks of French bread to get lots of cheesy fondue with every bite. "

Marinated Pineapple

24 appetizer servings

1   cup sugar
½   cup water

½   cup orange liqueur
½   cup lime juice
1   tablespoon grated orange rind
      (about 1 medium orange)

2   fresh pineapples, peeled, cored, and
      cubed

1 Combine sugar and water in a saucepan. Bring to a boil; cook 1 minute.

2 Add liqueur, lime juice, and orange rind; stir well.

3 Place cubed pineapple in a bowl. Pour sugar mixture over pineapple. Cover and chill at least 1 hour, stirring occasionally.

Perk Up Pineapple

Lime juice and orange liqueur tease these sweet pineapple chunks with tanginess. Set out some little decorative toothpicks so the gang can dig into the pineapple as appetizers, or spoon the syrupy chunks into small bowls for dessert. Most supermarkets have fresh pineapple already peeled and cored, so all you have to do is cube 'em!

Cucumber Sandwiches

about 3 dozen

3   tablespoons mayonnaise
⅛   teaspoon hot sauce
1   (8-ounce) package cream cheese,
          softened
1   (0.7-ounce) envelope Italian
          dressing mix

1   (12-ounce) loaf cocktail rye bread
1   large cucumber, thinly sliced (about
          36 slices)

1 Combine first 4 ingredients in a medium mixing bowl; beat at medium speed of an electric beater until smooth.

2 Spread cream cheese mixture over bread slices. Top each with a cucumber slice.

" These super-quick canapés were Mama's choice for teatime or to serve at her ladies' luncheons. Cocktail rye or pumpernickel slices are perfect bases for this kicky cheese mixture. If you want to get extra fancy, pull the tines of a fork down the cucumber before slicing it, and the slices will have pretty rippled edges. "

Popeye's Roll-ups

6 dozen

1 (10-ounce) package frozen chopped spinach, thawed and well drained
1 cup mayonnaise
1 (8-ounce) container sour cream
1 bunch green onions, chopped
1 (1-ounce) envelope Ranch-style dressing mix
1 (3-ounce) jar bacon bits

9 (10") flour tortillas

1 Combine first 6 ingredients, and stir mixture well.

2 Spread mixture on tortillas. Roll up, jellyroll fashion; wrap in plastic wrap. Chill 4 to 6 hours. Cut into ½"-thick slices.

> *Mama always said to eat your veggies. And what better way than in these tasty spinach roll-ups? I pumped up the flavor by adding a Ranch-style dressing mix and a jar of those crunchy little bacon bits.*

Hot Chili Peanuts

9 cups

9 cups salted dry-roasted peanuts
(about 2½ pounds)

6 tablespoons butter, melted
2 tablespoons ground red pepper
1 tablespoon chili powder
½ teaspoon salt

1 Preheat the oven to 350°. Spread peanuts in a single layer on an ungreased 10" x 15" rimmed baking sheet.

2 Combine butter and remaining 3 ingredients; stir well. Pour butter mixture over peanuts; toss gently. Bake at 350° for 15 minutes, stirring often.

Pass the Peanuts

Don't worry if you have only unsalted dry-roasted peanuts in your pantry; simply add 1 or 1½ tablespoons of salt instead of the ½ teaspoon called for in this recipe.

Cheesy Cocktail Muffins

4 dozen

¾ cup butter

2 cups (8 ounces) shredded sharp Cheddar cheese

2 cups self-rising flour

1 (8-ounce) container sour cream

2 tablespoons frozen chopped chives

1 Preheat the oven to 375°. Melt butter in a medium saucepan over medium heat. Add Cheddar cheese, and cook 2 minutes, stirring constantly. Stir in flour, sour cream, and chives.

2 Spoon batter into ungreased miniature (1¾") muffin pans, filling two-thirds full. Bake at 375° for 20 to 22 minutes. Remove muffins from pans immediately.

" These buttery little bites make great finger food for an appetizer buffet. If you have any muffins left after the party, they're the perfect companion with a bowl of hot soup or chili. And they freeze well, too!"

Sesame Cheese Wafers

2½ dozen

½   (15-ounce) package refrigerated
      piecrusts
1½ cups (6 ounces) shredded sharp
      Cheddar cheese
½   cup sesame seeds, toasted
½   teaspoon ground red pepper

1   to 2 teaspoons ice water

1 Preheat the oven to 450°. Process first 4 ingredients in a food processor bowl 30 seconds.

2 Add ice water (1 teaspoon at a time) through food chute with processor running; process just until dough begins to form a ball and leaves sides of bowl. Cover and chill 30 minutes.

3 Shape dough into 1" balls; place 2" apart on ungreased baking sheets. Flatten each ball in a crisscross pattern with a fork dipped in flour. Bake at 450° for 8 to 10 minutes or until lightly browned. Cool on wire racks.

> *" A refrigerated pie crust makes these wafers super easy to make. They don't hang around long when I have a party! If you don't have a food processor, just blend the ingredients with a pastry blender or two knives like you were making homemade pastry. Either way, they're a flaky sensation!"*

Pepperoni Pie Squares

8 to 10 appetizer servings

1 ½ cups all-purpose flour
2   cups milk
2   large eggs, lightly beaten
1   pound Muenster cheese, cubed
1   (8-ounce) package sliced pepperoni,
        chopped
1   teaspoon dried Italian seasoning

Pizza or marinara sauce

1 Preheat the oven to 350°. Combine first 6 ingredients; pour into a lightly greased 9" x 13" baking dish.

2 Bake at 350° for 30 minutes; cool slightly, and cut into squares. Serve with sauce.

66 These little pie squares are packed with a package of pepperoni and a whole pound of Muenster cheese! All you have to do is just mix and bake. Don't forget the pizza sauce for dipping. 99

Sesame Chicken Tenders

10 to 12 appetizer servings

2   pounds skinned and boned chicken
      breast halves

1   cup mayonnaise
2   teaspoons dried minced onion
2   teaspoons dry mustard
1   to 1½ cups crushed round buttery
      crackers
½   cup sesame seeds

1 Preheat the oven to 425°. Cut chicken into ¼" strips.

2 Stir together mayonnaise, onion, and mustard. Combine crackers and sesame seeds. Dip chicken into mayonnaise mixture; dredge in cracker mixture. Repeat procedure once.

3 Place chicken on a lightly greased baking sheet. Bake at 425° for 15 minutes or until done. Serve with your favorite honey-mustard sauce or barbecue sauce for dipping.

" Once you bite into these tender strips of crispy chicken, you'll forget the fast food variety. And the chicken strips are baked in the oven, so you don't have a mess in your kitchen from frying!"

Balsamic Chicken Wings

6 appetizer servings

2	pounds chicken wings
⅔	cup balsamic vinegar
3	green onions, thinly sliced

1 Cut off and discard chicken wing tips; cut wings in half at joint.

2 Combine chicken, vinegar, and green onions in a large heavy-duty, zip-top plastic bag. Seal bag, and shake gently. Marinate in refrigerator 8 hours, turning bag occasionally.

3 Preheat the grill. Remove chicken from marinade; discard marinade. Coat grill rack with nonstick cooking spray; place rack on grill over medium-high heat (350° to 400°). Place chicken on rack, and grill, covered, 8 to 10 minutes on each side or until done.

Just Wing It

To make this 3-ingredient recipe even easier, buy those wings in the supermarket that are already disjointed. You can find them in the frozen food section. No need to even thaw 'em—they'll thaw as they marinate.

Hot Cran-Apple Cider

13 cups

2 quarts apple cider
1½ quarts cranberry juice cocktail
¼ cup packed brown sugar
4 (3") cinnamon sticks
1½ teaspoons whole cloves
2 lemons, thinly sliced and divided

1 Combine first 5 ingredients and half of lemon slices in a large Dutch oven. Bring to a boil; reduce heat, and simmer, uncovered, 15 minutes. Remove and discard cinnamon sticks, cloves, and lemon slices.

2 Pour beverage into cups. Top each serving with 1 of the remaining lemon slices. Serve hot.

I put on a pot of this cider any time company's coming over in the winter. The spices fill the air and the hot cider warms the soul.

Peachy Tea

4 cups

2½ cups peach nectar
2 honey and lemon tea bags

1 (10-ounce) bottle club soda, chilled

1 Combine peach nectar and tea bags in a glass jar; cover tightly, and shake vigorously. Chill at least 8 hours.

2 Remove and discard tea bags. Add club soda to peach nectar mixture just before serving; stir gently. Serve over ice.

Flavored tea bags infuse sweet peach nectar with honey and lemon tastes, while fizzy club soda lends pizzazz—this tea is the perfect refresher for those hot summer days.

Lemon Honeyade

1 ¼ cups

1   cup water
2   tablespoons fresh lemon juice
3   tablespoons honey

1 Combine water, lemon juice, and honey in a glass; serve over ice.

It's as Simple as 1, 2, 3
Here's a great recipe when you're craving fresh lemonade because you make it by the glass, and the recipe is so easy to remember—1, 2, 3! Simply multiply the ingredients if you want to keep a stash in the fridge.

PB 'n' Nanner Shake

3 cups

¾ cup milk
2 cups vanilla ice cream
1 small banana, cut into 1" pieces
1 tablespoon creamy peanut butter

1 Process all ingredients in container of an electric blender until smooth, stopping once to scrape down sides. Serve immediately.

Lighten Up

If you're watching your waistline, just substitute fat-free milk for regular milk, ice milk or frozen yogurt for ice cream, and reduced-fat peanut butter spread for the peanut butter. You'll still get that creamy peanut butter taste in every sip!

Parson's Piña Colada

2¾ cups

½ cup pineapple juice
¼ cup cream of coconut
2 cups vanilla ice cream

1 Process all ingredients in container of an electric blender until smooth, stopping once to scrape down sides. Serve immediately.

"Soothing vanilla ice cream enhances the refreshing tropical flavors of my nonalcoholic piña colada. You'll think you're on an island somewhere."

Holiday Nog

6 quarts

3   (½-gallon) cartons vanilla ice cream,
     softened

1   (750-milliliter) bottle brandy
½   (750-milliliter) bottle coffee liqueur
     (about 1 ½ cups)
Ground nutmeg

1 Spoon softened ice cream into a punch bowl; stir with a spoon until ice cream is smooth.

2 Pour brandy and coffee liqueur over ice cream. Stir gently just until blended. (Do not overstir; nog will be too foamy.) Sprinkle with nutmeg.

❝Toast the holidays with my special nog that's full of spirit! Remember that it's for adults only—it's made with a whole bottle of brandy!❞

29

Frozen Mango Daiquiri

5 cups

2   small ripe mangoes (about 1
      pound), peeled and cut into
      chunks
½   cup dark or light rum
¼   to ½ cup sugar
¼   cup fresh lime juice
¼   teaspoon ground ginger

Ice cubes

Lime wedges
Sugar

1 Process first 5 ingredients in container of an electric blender until smooth, stopping once to scrape down sides.

2 Add ice to 4¾-cup level on blender container; process until mixture is thick and slushy.

3 To decorate the glasses, rub a lime wedge around the rim of each glass. Place sugar in a shallow bowl, and spin the rim of each glass in sugar.

Mango Know-How
The sweetness of mangoes will vary with each season, so you may need to vary the amount of sugar with the season. To cut a mango, slice the fruit in half, cutting around the big seed in the center. Then score the flesh into squares and slice it.

Fancy Schmancy Dinners

"Having company or planning a special dinner for your family? The gang'll be all smiles when you bring these dishes to the table. But let's keep it our secret how easy these recipes are!"

Sweet-and-Sour Apricot Chicken

4 servings

2 tablespoons peanut oil

4 skinned and boned chicken breast
   halves, cut into 2" pieces

6 fresh apricots, halved or 12 canned
   apricot halves

1⅓ cups sweet-and-sour sauce

3 green onions, thinly sliced

1 Heat oil in a large skillet or wok over medium-high heat. Add chicken; cook 10 minutes, stirring often. Add apricot halves; cook 1 minute, stirring constantly. Add sweet-and-sour sauce; cook, stirring constantly, until thoroughly heated.

2 Sprinkle chicken with green onions. Serve over rice.

So Fast and So Fine!

Experiment with different sweet-and-sour sauces on the market to find your favorite brand. Then stir it into this dish for a tangy-sweet sensation!

Chicken with Artichoke Cream Sauce

4 servings

4   skinned and boned chicken breast
     halves
5   tablespoons all-purpose flour,
     divided
¼   cup butter, divided

1   (6-ounce) jar marinated
     quartered artichoke hearts,
     undrained

1   cup milk

1 Place chicken between 2 sheets of heavy-duty plastic wrap, and flatten to ¼" thickness, using a meat mallet or rolling pin. Dredge chicken in 2 tablespoons flour. Melt 2 tablespoons butter in a large skillet over medium heat; add chicken, and cook 5 minutes on each side or until done. Transfer chicken to a serving platter; set aside, and keep warm.

2 Drain artichoke hearts, reserving liquid. Set artichoke hearts and liquid aside.

3 Melt remaining 2 tablespoons butter in a heavy saucepan over low heat; add remaining 3 tablespoons flour, stirring until mixture is smooth. Cook 1 minute, stirring constantly. Gradually add milk and reserved artichoke liquid; cook over medium heat, stirring constantly, until mixture is thickened and bubbly. Stir in artichoke hearts; pour mixture over chicken. Serve with rice.

" Shhh—it's the marinade from the jar of artichoke hearts that gives this cream sauce its rich flavor. "

33

Praline Chicken

6 servings

2   teaspoons Creole seasoning
6   skinned and boned chicken breast halves
5   tablespoons butter, melted

1/3 cup maple syrup
2   tablespoons brown sugar
1   cup chopped pecans, toasted

1 Sprinkle Creole seasoning on both sides of chicken. Cook chicken in butter in a large skillet over medium heat 4 to 5 minutes on each side or until done. Remove chicken, reserving drippings in skillet. Place chicken on a serving platter; set aside, and keep warm.

2 Add maple syrup and sugar to drippings in skillet; bring to a boil. Stir in pecans, and cook 1 minute or until thoroughly heated. Spoon pecan mixture over chicken.

Flavor to the Max!

Toast your pecans in an oven or a skillet to enhance their flavor before stirring up this spicy praline topping. To toast pecans, spread them on a lightly greased rimmed baking sheet. Bake at 350°, stirring occasionally, 5 to 8 minutes.

Chicken Marsala

4 servings

4	skinned and boned chicken breast halves
1	large egg, lightly beaten
¼	cup all-purpose flour
2	tablespoons butter, melted

1 Dip chicken in egg, and dredge in flour. Brown chicken in butter in a large skillet over medium-high heat. Remove chicken, reserving drippings in skillet; set chicken aside.

2	cups sliced fresh mushrooms
1	cup Marsala (see note below)
½	teaspoon salt
¼	teaspoon pepper

2 Cook mushrooms in drippings in skillet over medium-high heat, stirring constantly, until tender. Add chicken, Marsala, salt, and pepper; cook until heated.

Quick Change

Rich, smoky-flavored Marsala really dresses up chicken breasts. But if you don't have Marsala on hand, you can substitute 1 cup dry white wine and 1 tablespoon plus 1 teaspoon brandy.

Slow-and-Easy Asian Chicky

(pictured on facing page)
6 servings

3½ pounds chicken breast halves and thighs, skinned
1 teaspoon garlic salt
¼ teaspoon pepper

1 cup chicken broth
½ teaspoon ground ginger
1 (8½-ounce) can sliced pineapple in heavy syrup, undrained
1 (8-ounce) can sliced water chestnuts, drained

4 green onions, diagonally sliced
¼ cup soy sauce
1 tablespoon white vinegar
¼ cup cornstarch
Chow mein noodles

1 Sprinkle chicken pieces with garlic salt and pepper; place in a 5-quart electric slow cooker.

2 Combine chicken broth and ginger, stirring well. Drain pineapple, reserving syrup. Add syrup to broth mixture, stirring well; cut pineapple slices into fourths. Arrange pineapple and water chestnuts over chicken. Pour broth mixture over chicken. Cover and cook on HIGH setting 1 hour; reduce heat to LOW, and cook 6 to 7 more hours.

3 Add green onions to mixture in slow cooker. Combine soy sauce, vinegar, and cornstarch, stirring until smooth. Stir into broth mixture, gently moving chicken pieces. Cover and cook on HIGH setting 10 minutes or until slightly thickened. Serve with chow mein noodles.

The slow cooker is the answer to a busy person's prayers—boy, do I know that! Remember: If you're cooking any type of meat, cook it on HIGH setting for 1 hour before reducing it to LOW setting to properly heat ingredients to the necessary temperature.

Mighty Meatball Sandwiches, page 76

Louisiana Baked Shrimp, page 86

Chicken Manicotti with Chive Cream Sauce

(pictured on facing page)
6 servings

1 (1-pound) package manicotti shells

2 (8-ounce) containers soft cream
   cheese with chives and onions
⅔ cup milk
¼ cup grated Parmesan cheese

2 cups diced cooked chicken
1 (10-ounce) package frozen chopped
   broccoli, thawed and drained
1 (4-ounce) jar diced pimiento,
   drained
¼ teaspoon pepper
Paprika

1 Cook pasta according to package directions, including salt; drain well.

2 Meanwhile, place cream cheese in a saucepan, and cook over medium-low heat until cheese melts. Slowly add milk, stirring until smooth. Add Parmesan cheese, stirring well.

3 Preheat the oven to 350°. Combine ¾ cup cream sauce, chicken, and next 3 ingredients in a large bowl. Carefully stuff about ⅓ cup filling into 12 manicotti shells, discarding any shells that split. Arrange shells in an ungreased 9" x 13" baking dish. Pour remaining cream sauce over shells. Sprinkle with paprika. Cover and bake at 350° for 30 minutes.

" Streamlined is the buzzword for this manicotti—I use chive cream cheese in the sauce, and frozen diced chicken and broccoli in the filling. Try my trick to fill the shells quickly and cleanly. Just spoon the filling into a heavy-duty, zip-top plastic bag, seal it, and snip a hole in one corner to "pipe" the filling into the shells—it's OOH SO EASY! "

Easy Beef Tenderloin

8 to 10 servings

6   green onions, chopped
½   cup butter, melted
3   beef bouillon cubes
2   tablespoons red wine vinegar

1   (5- to 6-pound) beef tenderloin, trimmed

1 Cook green onions in butter in a small saucepan over medium-high heat, stirring constantly, until tender; add bouillon cubes, stirring until dissolved. Remove from heat, and stir in vinegar.

2 Preheat the oven to 425°. Place tenderloin in a large shallow dish. Spoon butter mixture over tenderloin; cover with aluminum foil, and let stand 15 minutes.

3 Place tenderloin on a rack in a roasting pan; insert meat thermometer into thickest part of tenderloin. Bake at 425° for 30 to 45 minutes or until thermometer registers 145° (medium-rare) or 160° (medium). Let stand 10 minutes before slicing.

❝ Beef tenderloin is fabulous enough to stand by itself, but my four secret ingredients enhance the flavor even more! Your family will be all smiles when you bring this platter to the table! ❞

Grilled Porterhouse Steaks

4 servings

¼ cup olive oil
2 tablespoons minced fresh basil
4 cloves garlic, crushed
2 (2-pound) porterhouse steaks
1 tablespoon seasoned salt
1 tablespoon freshly ground pepper

1 Preheat the grill. Combine first 3 ingredients in a small bowl. Rub oil mixture on both sides of steaks; sprinkle with seasoned salt and pepper.

2 Grill, covered, over medium-high heat (350° to 400°) 10 minutes on each side or to desired degree of doneness.

" My porterhouse steaks rival those at the best steakhouses. Prove it by inviting a few friends over. Then rub my mixture of fresh basil, garlic, and olive oil over these juicy steaks, sprinkle 'em liberally with seasoned salt and pepper—and before you know it, m-m-m good! "

Beef Fillets au Vin

4 servings

4   (8-ounce) beef tenderloin steaks
      (1½" thick)
½   teaspoon salt, divided
½   teaspoon pepper, divided
3   tablespoons butter, divided

1   tablespoon minced shallot or onion
2   cloves garlic, minced, or 1 teaspoon
      garlic powder
1   pound fresh mushrooms, thinly
      sliced
½   cup dry red wine

1 Sprinkle steaks with ¼ teaspoon salt and ¼ teaspoon pepper. Melt 1 tablespoon butter in a large skillet over medium heat. Add steaks; cook 7 to 9 minutes on each side or to desired degree of doneness. Remove from skillet; set aside, and keep warm.

2 Melt 1 tablespoon butter in skillet over medium-high heat; add shallot, garlic, and mushrooms; sauté until tender. Stir in ½ cup wine, and cook over medium-high heat 5 minutes or until wine is reduced by half. Add remaining 1 tablespoon butter, ¼ teaspoon salt, and ¼ teaspoon pepper, stirring until butter melts. Serve steaks with mushroom-wine sauce.

> **"**Vin is French for wine, and I stir half a cup of it into the mushroom sauce for this recipe! Then I reduce the sauce, spoon it over each fillet, and enjoy the rest of the bottle of wine with dinner!**"**

Sirloin Tips with Garlic Butter

6 servings

2 cups butter, softened
4 cloves garlic, minced
¼ cup dry white wine
1 tablespoon chopped fresh parsley

1 large onion, sliced
1 (8-ounce) package sliced fresh mushrooms

1½ pounds sirloin steak, cut into 1-inch pieces
Salt and pepper
2 tablespoons dry sherry

1 Combine first 4 ingredients; stir garlic butter well.

2 Melt 3 tablespoons garlic butter in a large skillet over medium-high heat. Add onion, and cook 6 minutes or until golden. Add mushrooms, and cook, stirring constantly, 5 minutes or until tender. Remove onion mixture from skillet. Set aside.

3 Sprinkle steak liberally with salt and pepper. Melt 3 tablespoons garlic butter in skillet over medium-high heat; add steak. Cook 5 minutes or to desired degree of doneness, stirring constantly. Return onion mixture to skillet. Stir in sherry. Cook, stirring constantly, until thoroughly heated. Serve over hot cooked noodles.

"My savory garlic butter makes more than enough for these tasty beef tips. Roll the extra butter into logs to slice and top steamed fresh veggies to serve on the side. To do so, spoon butter mixture onto a sheet of wax paper. Wrap in wax paper, and chill at least 30 minutes or until slightly firm. Roll butter in wax paper, back and forth, to make a log. Chill up to 2 days. You can also freeze butter logs."

Veal Parmigiana

4 servings

1 pound veal cutlets
¼ teaspoon salt
¼ teaspoon pepper
¼ cup all-purpose flour

¼ cup butter, melted and divided
2 (8-ounce) cans tomato sauce with
    roasted garlic

1 (8-ounce) package sliced mozzarella
    cheese
Grated Parmesan cheese

Mama mia—this tastes just like what Mama used to make! It's so easy, and you can even use skinned and boned chicken breast halves instead of veal, if you'd like.

1 Place veal between 2 sheets of heavy-duty plastic wrap, and flatten to ⅛" thickness, using a meat mallet or rolling pin. Sprinkle with salt and pepper, and dredge in flour.

2 Brown half of veal in 2 tablespoons butter in a large skillet over medium-high heat 3 minutes on each side. Remove veal, reserving drippings in skillet. Place veal in a lightly greased 9" x 13" broiler-proof baking dish. Repeat procedure with remaining veal and 2 tablespoons butter, reserving drippings in skillet. Add tomato sauce to drippings in skillet; stir well. Bring to a boil over medium heat, stirring occasionally.

3 Meanwhile, place cheese slices on veal, and preheat the broiler. Broil veal 5½" from heat 1 minute or until cheese melts. Spoon sauce over veal, and sprinkle with Parmesan cheese. Serve immediately.

Pecan-Crusted Lamb Chops

4 servings

1	egg white, lightly beaten
1	tablespoon Dijon mustard

1 Combine egg white and mustard, stirring well. Set aside.

⅓	cup finely chopped pecans
¼	cup fine, dry breadcrumbs (store-bought)
1	small clove garlic, minced
4	(1"-thick) lamb loin chops

2 Combine pecans, breadcrumbs, and garlic; stir well. Dip lamb chops in egg white mixture, and dredge in pecan mixture, coating well.

2	tablespoons vegetable oil

3 Cook lamb chops in oil in a medium skillet over medium-low heat 7 to 10 minutes on each side or to desired degree of doneness.

" When friends are coming to dinner and I want to treat them to something special, I turn to these pecan-studded lamb chops. When you're at the supermarket, look for lamb that has bright pink meat, pink bones, and white fat to make sure you're getting the freshest meat available. "

Garlic Lover's Pork Loin

8 to 10 servings

1 (3- to 4-pound) boneless pork loin
    roast
5 cloves garlic, cut into ⅛" slices

1 (8-ounce) bottle Italian salad
    dressing
1 cup dry white wine
10 black peppercorns, crushed

1 Cut ½" slits at 1" intervals in diagonal rows on top of roast. Insert a garlic sliver into each slit.

2 Combine salad dressing, wine, and peppercorns in a large heavy-duty, zip-top plastic bag. Reserve ½ cup dressing mixture in refrigerator for basting during grilling. Add roast to remaining mixture in bag; seal bag, and chill 8 hours, turning bag occasionally. Remove roast from marinade, discarding marinade.

3 Preheat the grill. Coat a grill rack with nonstick cooking spray, and place over medium-high heat (350° to 400°); place roast on rack. Grill, covered, 35 minutes or until meat thermometer inserted into thickest part reaches 160°, turning and basting with reserved ½ cup dressing mixture after 20 minutes.

Too Rainy to Grill Out?

This roast tastes just as fabulous cooked in your oven. Just place the roast, fat side up, in a shallow roasting pan. Bake, uncovered, at 325° for 1 hour and 20 minutes or until a meat thermometer inserted into thickest part registers 160°, turning and basting with reserved ½ cup dressing mixture after 30 minutes.

Pork Tenderloin with Orange Sauce

4 servings

1½ tablespoons coarse-grained mustard
1 clove garlic, minced
¼ teaspoon chopped fresh or dried rosemary
⅛ teaspoon freshly ground pepper

2 (8-ounce) pork tenderloins
¼ cup low-sugar orange marmalade, divided

¼ cup chicken broth

1 Preheat the oven to 400°. Combine first 4 ingredients in a small bowl; stir well, and set aside.

2 Slice each tenderloin lengthwise to, but not through, the center, leaving bottom half connected; gently press each side to lie flat. Spread mustard mixture evenly onto cut side of each tenderloin. Fold tenderloin together over mustard mixture; tie securely with string at 2" intervals. Place tenderloins, seam side down, on a lightly greased rack in a roasting pan. Brush each with 1 table-spoon marmalade. Bake, uncovered, at 400° for 35 minutes or until a meat ther-mometer inserted into thickest part of tenderloins registers 160°.

3 Combine remaining 2 tablespoons marmalade and chicken broth in a small saucepan. Bring to a boil; reduce heat, and simmer, uncovered, 2 to 3 minutes or until thickened. To serve, slice tenderloins, and arrange on a serving platter. Spoon marmalade mixture over slices.

" I'm not exactly trying to cut calories in this dish by using low-sugar marmalade, but you do have that as a bonus! Low-sugar marmalade lets you roast the pork at a high temperature to keep it juicy while ensuring that the marmalade glaze doesn't burn."

Pork Medallions with Mustard Sauce

4 servings

1	(1-pound) pork tenderloin
½	teaspoon salt, divided
¼	teaspoon pepper
1	tablespoon vegetable oil
½	cup half-and-half
2	tablespoons Dijon mustard
3	green onions, sliced

1 Cut pork into 1"-thick slices. Place slices between 2 sheets of heavy-duty plastic wrap, and flatten to ¼" thickness, using a meat mallet or rolling pin.

2 Sprinkle pork with ¼ teaspoon salt and the pepper. Cook half of pork medallions in hot oil in a large nonstick skillet 2 minutes on each side or until browned. Remove pork from skillet; set aside, and keep warm. Repeat procedure with remaining half of pork.

3 Reduce heat to low; add half-and-half to skillet, stirring constantly, scraping particles that cling to bottom. Stir in mustard, green onions, and remaining ¼ teaspoon salt. Return pork to skillet; cover and cook 2 minutes, turning to coat with sauce.

" To lap up every drop of the luscious mustard sauce, I always serve these tender pork medallions over rice. "

Prosciutto with Angel Hair

6 servings

2   (9-ounce) packages refrigerated
     angel hair pasta

3   tablespoons butter
¼   pound prosciutto, cut into very thin
     strips
1   (16-ounce) jar Alfredo sauce
1   cup freshly grated Parmesan cheese,
     divided
¼   teaspoon freshly ground pepper

1 Prepare pasta according to package directions, omitting salt; drain. Return pasta to pan, and keep warm.

2 Meanwhile, melt butter in a large skillet over medium heat. Add prosciutto and Alfredo sauce; cook until heated. Stir in ⅓ cup cheese and the pepper. Pour sauce over pasta; toss well. Sprinkle with remaining ⅔ cup cheese. Serve immediately.

" Prosciutto, the spicy Italian ham, tastes great just by itself, served with melons or figs as a classic first course, or dished up in a creamy cheese sauce over pasta as I've done here. Try it— you'll love it! "

Flounder au Gratin

4 servings

2½ pounds (½"-thick) flounder fillets
3   tablespoons lemon juice

¼   cup fine, dry breadcrumbs (regular or herb seasoned)
¼   cup grated Parmesan cheese
3   tablespoons butter, cut into small pieces

1 Preheat the oven to 375°. Arrange flounder in a buttered 9" x 13" baking dish; drizzle with lemon juice.

2 Combine breadcrumbs and cheese in a small bowl. Sprinkle breadcrumb mixture over flounder; dot with butter.

3 Bake, uncovered, at 375° for 30 minutes or until fish flakes easily when tested with a fork. Serve immediately, using a slotted spatula.

Fishin' for More

"Floundering" for ideas for what to do with this mild fish? Four staple ingredients keep it simple, and your family will clamor for more!

Oriental Grouper

4 servings

Garlic-flavored vegetable cooking spray
4   (4-ounce) grouper fillets (or red
       snapper or halibut)

⅓   cup soy sauce
⅓   cup dry sherry
1   tablespoon brown sugar
¾   teaspoon ground ginger

2   green onions, sliced

66 I just love the flavored nonstick cooking sprays because they do two jobs at once—flavor the food and grease the pan. The spray helps cook up this grouper in a snap! 99

1 Place a large nonstick skillet coated with nonstick cooking spray over medium-high heat until hot. Add fillets, and cook 4 minutes on each side; remove fillets from skillet, and keep warm.

2 Combine soy sauce, sherry, sugar, and ginger; add mixture to hot skillet. Cook over high heat 3 minutes or until mixture thickens, stirring constantly to loosen particles that cling to bottom of skillet.

3 Return fillets to skillet, turning to coat with glaze. Transfer fillets to individual serving plates; sprinkle green onions evenly over fish, and serve immediately.

Savory Salmon Steaks

4 servings

4   (8-ounce) salmon steaks (1" thick)
3   tablespoons dark brown sugar
3   tablespoons prepared horseradish
3   tablespoons Dijon mustard
3   tablespoons vegetable oil
3   tablespoons soy sauce

1 Place steaks in a large shallow dish. Combine brown sugar and remaining 4 ingredients; cover and chill half of brown sugar mixture for basting. Brush remaining half over steaks. Cover and marinate in refrigerator up to 6 hours.

2 Preheat the grill. Remove steaks from dish, discarding marinade; place in a greased grilling basket. Grill, covered, over medium-high heat (350° to 400°) 5 minutes on each side or until fish flakes easily when tested with a fork, basting often with reserved marinade.

A Tisket, a Tasket . . .

Bring out the grill basket! Fish sometimes sticks when cooked directly on the grill rack, even using nonstick cooking spray. But the grill basket does the job nicely! And you don't want to miss a single bite!

Oven-Roasted Scallops

4 servings

1½ pounds sea scallops (about 24)

1 large egg
1 tablespoon water
½ cup Italian-seasoned breadcrumbs
¼ teaspoon salt
¼ teaspoon fennel seeds, crushed (optional)

2 tablespoons butter, melted
1 tablespoon lemon juice

1 Preheat the oven to 450°. Rinse scallops, and pat dry with paper towels to remove excess moisture.

2 Combine egg and water in a bowl; stir well. Combine breadcrumbs, salt, and fennel seeds, if desired. Dip each scallop into egg mixture; dredge in breadcrumb mixture.

3 Place scallops on a lightly greased 10" x 15" rimmed baking sheet. Drizzle scallops with melted butter and lemon juice. Bake, uncovered, at 450° for 15 to 20 minutes or until scallops are golden.

Seaworthy
Because they're larger in diameter than bay scallops, sea scallops work best in this recipe that cooks 'em up nice 'n' brown! You'll find fresh sea scallops in the seafood department, or look for 'em in the frozen foods section of your supermarket.

Garlic-Skewered 'n' Grilled Shrimp

6 servings

21   large cloves garlic
⅓   cup olive oil
¼   cup pizza sauce
2   tablespoons red wine vinegar
½   teaspoon ground red pepper
24   jumbo fresh shrimp, peeled and
      deveined (2 pounds unpeeled)

1 Mince 3 cloves garlic. Combine minced garlic, olive oil, and remaining 4 ingredients in a medium bowl, stirring well. Cover and marinate in refrigerator 30 minutes. Cover remaining garlic cloves with water in a small saucepan. Bring to a boil, and boil 3 minutes; drain well, and set aside.

2 Preheat the grill. Remove shrimp from marinade, reserving marinade. Bring marinade to a boil in a small saucepan; set aside. Thread shrimp and garlic evenly onto 6 (10") metal skewers. Grill, covered, over medium-high heat (350° to 400°) 3 to 4 minutes on each side or until shrimp turn pink, basting with reserved marinade.

Garlic in All Its Glory!

Whole cloves of garlic line up like little soldiers between the shrimp on these kabobs, mellowing out as they cook and providing aroma and flavor that will call your family to dinner.

Shrimp with Jalapeño-Orange Sauce

4 servings

¼ cup butter
24 large fresh shrimp, peeled and deveined (about 1½ pounds unpeeled)

2 tablespoons minced shallot
1 to 2 small jalapeño peppers, seeded and finely chopped
½ cup dry white wine
1½ cups orange juice
¾ cup heavy whipping cream
¼ teaspoon salt

1 Melt butter in a large skillet over medium-high heat. Add shrimp, and cook just until shrimp turn pink. Remove from skillet; set aside, and keep warm.

2 Add shallot and jalapeño peppers to skillet; cook over medium-high heat 1 minute, stirring constantly. Add wine, and bring to a boil. Stir in orange juice, cream, and salt; return to a boil. Cook over high heat about 10 minutes or until mixture is thickened, stirring occasionally.

3 Return shrimp to sauce, and cook just until thoroughly heated. Serve with rice or pasta.

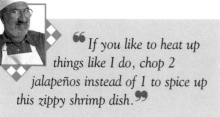

If you like to heat up things like I do, chop 2 jalapeños instead of 1 to spice up this zippy shrimp dish.

Lasagna-Chicken Florentine

4 servings

2¾ cups bottled Alfredo sauce
⅛ teaspoon ground nutmeg

6 no-boil lasagna noodles
1½ cups shredded cooked chicken
    breast (about 6 ounces)
1 (10-ounce) package frozen chopped
    spinach, thawed, drained, and
    squeezed dry
½ teaspoon freshly ground pepper,
    divided
1½ cups (6 ounces) shredded pizza-
    blend cheese or Cheddar cheese

1 Preheat the oven to 450°. Combine Alfredo sauce and nutmeg.

2 Spread ½ cup sauce mixture in a lightly greased 8" square baking dish. Arrange 2 noodles over sauce; top with half of chicken and half of spinach. Sprinkle with ¼ teaspoon pepper; top with ¾ cup sauce and ½ cup cheese. Repeat layers, ending with noodles.

3 Spread remaining sauce over noodles. Cover with aluminum foil sprayed with nonstick cooking spray, and bake at 450° for 25 minutes or until noodles are tender and sauce is bubbly. Uncover and top with remaining ½ cup cheese; bake 5 more minutes. Let stand 5 minutes before serving.

" Lasagna typically takes longer to put together than it does to cook. Precooked noodles and prepackaged convenience products make my version a zip to prepare! "

Pasta with Tomatoes, Brie, and Basil

(pictured on page 2)
8 servings

1	(15-ounce) round Brie

4 large ripe tomatoes, chopped
½ cup olive oil
1 cup julienne-sliced fresh basil
3 cloves garlic, minced
½ teaspoon salt
⅛ teaspoon pepper

1½ pounds dried linguine, uncooked
½ cup freshly grated Parmesan cheese

1 Remove rind from Brie, and cut Brie into ½" cubes.

2 Combine Brie, tomatoes, and next 5 ingredients; toss well. Let stand at room temperature at least 2 hours.

3 Cook pasta according to package directions, including salt. Drain pasta, and toss with fresh tomato sauce. Top with Parmesan cheese.

" This vegetarian main dish is to die for! It calls for julienne-sliced (thin slivers) fresh basil, which is easier to do than it sounds! Just roll several large basil leaves together, and thinly slice the roll crosswise. That's all there is to it!"

Two-Cheese Penne with Nutty Cream Sauce

6 servings

16   ounces uncooked penne pasta

1   bunch green onions, chopped
1   cup coarsely chopped walnuts
¼   cup olive oil

4   ounces goat cheese, crumbled
1   cup whipping cream
½   cup freshly grated Romano cheese
Freshly ground pepper to taste

1 Cook penne pasta according to package directions, including salt; drain well, and set aside.

2 Cook green onions and walnuts in oil in a large skillet over medium-high heat, stirring constantly, until green onions are tender.

3 Add pasta and goat cheese to onion mixture; reduce heat, and cook, stirring constantly, until cheese melts. Remove from heat. Stir in cream, Romano cheese, and pepper to taste; toss gently. Serve immediately.

A Grate Tip!

To save preparation time for this dish, look for freshly grated Romano cheese in the specialty cheese section of your grocery store. Or you can grate your own cheese when you have time, and keep it on hand in the freezer.

Easy Weeknight Suppers

"Suppers are a cinch when you pick one of these easy, breezy favorites."

Chicken Piccata

4 servings

1	large egg
3	tablespoons lemon juice, divided

1/3	cup all-purpose flour
1/8	teaspoon garlic powder
4	skinned and boned chicken breast halves
1/4	cup butter, melted

2	teaspoons chicken-flavored bouillon granules
1/2	cup hot water

1 Combine egg and 1 tablespoon lemon juice in a small bowl; beat well with a wire whisk.

2 Combine flour and garlic powder in a small bowl; stir well. Dip chicken in egg mixture; dredge in flour mixture. Brown chicken in butter in a large skillet over medium-high heat 4 to 5 minutes on each side.

3 Dissolve bouillon granules in hot water; add bouillon mixture and remaining 2 tablespoons lemon juice to chicken. Bring to a boil; cover, reduce heat, and simmer 20 minutes or until chicken is done. Serve over warm cooked rice, if desired.

Pucker Up!
Using fresh lemon juice will make this chicken recipe extra special. See for yourself!

Easy Chicken Divan

6 servings

2	(10-ounce) packages frozen broccoli spears
6	skinned and boned chicken breast halves
2	(10¾-ounce) cans cream of chicken soup, undiluted
½	cup (2 ounces) shredded sharp Cheddar cheese
½	cup mayonnaise
½	teaspoon curry powder
½	cup fine, dry breadcrumbs (store-bought)
2	tablespoons butter, melted

1 Preheat the oven to 350°. Cook broccoli according to package directions; drain. Place in a greased 9" x 13" baking dish; top with chicken. Set aside.

2 Combine soup and next 3 ingredients in a medium saucepan; cook over medium heat, stirring constantly, until cheese melts. Pour over chicken and broccoli. Sprinkle with breadcrumbs; drizzle butter over breadcrumbs. Bake, uncovered, at 350° for 40 minutes or until chicken is done.

Who doesn't love this classic with its rich, creamy sauce? No one will ever guess you used canned soup to whip up this casserole! OOH IT'S SO GOOD!!

Garlic-Lime Chicken-on-the-Grill

4 servings

½   cup soy sauce
¼   cup fresh lime juice
1   tablespoon Worcestershire sauce
½   teaspoon coarsely ground pepper
2   cloves garlic, minced
4   skinned and boned chicken breast
      halves

1 Combine first 5 ingredients in a large heavy-duty, zip-top plastic bag. Add chicken. Seal bag; marinate in refrigerator 30 minutes, turning bag once.

2 Preheat the grill. Remove chicken from marinade, discarding marinade. Coat grill rack with nonstick cooking spray; place rack on grill over medium-high heat (350° to 400°). Place chicken on rack, and grill 5 to 6 minutes on each side or until done.

“ Just a short soak in a zingy marinade infuses this grilled chicken with flavor you're gonna love!”

Baked Chicken Nuggets

4 servings

½ cup fine, dry breadcrumbs
  (store-bought)

¼ cup grated Parmesan cheese

½ teaspoon dried basil

½ teaspoon dried thyme

¼ teaspoon salt

4 skinned and boned chicken breast
  halves, cut into 1" pieces

¼ cup butter, melted

1 Combine first 5 ingredients in a large heavy-duty, zip-top plastic bag; seal bag, and shake well.

2 Preheat the oven to 400°. Dip chicken in butter, and shake, a few pieces at a time, in breadcrumb mixture. Place chicken on a greased baking sheet. Bake at 400° for 20 minutes or until browned.

❝ Kids will gobble up these crispy homemade chicken nuggets, especially with a few squirts of ketchup. ❞

Chunky Chicken-Noodle Casserole

6 servings

8   ounces medium egg noodles,
       uncooked

½   cup butter
⅓   cup all-purpose flour
2   cups chicken broth
1   cup milk
2   teaspoons seasoned salt

2   cups chopped cooked chicken
1   (4-ounce) can sliced mushrooms,
       drained
⅓   cup grated Parmesan cheese

1 Cook noodles according to package directions, omitting salt; drain and set aside in a large bowl.

2 Preheat the oven to 350°. Melt butter in a medium saucepan over low heat; gradually add flour, stirring until smooth. Cook 1 minute, stirring constantly. Gradually add chicken broth and milk; cook over medium heat, stirring constantly, until mixture is slightly thickened and bubbly. Stir in seasoned salt; set aside.

3 Combine noodles, chicken, and mushrooms; stir in sauce. Spoon mixture into a lightly greased 9" x 13" baking dish; sprinkle with cheese. Bake, uncovered, at 350° for 20 minutes or until thoroughly heated.

❝Use your noodle! Next time you're invited to a potluck supper, wow the crowd with this noodle casserole filled with chicken chunks.❞

One-Pot Chicken Dinner

4 servings

1   (16-ounce) can chow mein
     vegetables, drained
1   (10¾-ounce) can chicken and rice
     soup, undiluted
1   (10¾-ounce) can cream of chicken
     soup, undiluted
1   cup chopped cooked chicken
2   tablespoons soy sauce

1   (3-ounce) can chow mein noodles

1 Preheat the oven to 350°. Combine first 5 ingredients in a large bowl; stir well. Spoon into a well-greased 7" x 11" baking dish.

2 Sprinkle with chow mein noodles. Bake, uncovered, at 350° for 25 minutes or until hot and bubbly. Serve immediately.

66 You know I'm a big fan of convenience products. If you're like me, you'll stock a few of these convenience items in your pantry so you'll have everything you need to stir up this easy entrée when you have leftover chicken in the fridge. 99

Chicken Livers in Sour Cream

4 servings

½   cup butter
1½ cups sliced fresh mushrooms
1   large onion, sliced or chopped
1   pound chicken livers

1   (8-ounce) carton sour cream
⅓   cup dry sherry
¼   teaspoon salt
⅛   teaspoon pepper

1 Melt butter in a large skillet over low heat. Add mushrooms and onion; cook over medium-high heat, stirring constantly, until vegetables are tender. Add livers, and cook 1 minute. Cover, reduce heat to low, and cook 15 minutes.

2 Stir in sour cream and remaining 3 ingredients, and cook until thoroughly heated. Serve immediately over warm cooked rice or in puff pastry shells.

❝ These chicken livers are full of old-time flavor. I like to serve 'em over rice. But if you wanna get fancy, spoon 'em into puff pastry shells. ❞

Classy Turkey Cutlets

4 servings

1   pound turkey breast cutlets
½   teaspoon salt
½   teaspoon ground white pepper
¼   cup vegetable oil
¾   cup all-purpose flour
2   large eggs, lightly beaten

1   avocado, peeled and sliced
1   tomato, sliced
1   (6-ounce) package sliced mozzarella
      cheese

1 Preheat the oven to Broil. Sprinkle turkey cutlets with salt and pepper. Heat oil in a large skillet over medium-high heat. Dredge cutlets in flour; dip in egg, and dredge again in flour. Add cutlets to skillet, and cook until browned. Remove turkey cutlets from skillet, and place on a rack in a broiler pan.

2 Arrange avocado and tomato slices evenly on top of cutlets. Top with cheese slices. Broil 5½" from heat 5 minutes or until cheese melts.

" Take a break from chicken and try my turkey cutlets for a change of pace. Dress 'em up with avocado, tomato, and cheese for a classy touch. "

Easy Asian Beef and Noodles

2 servings

½   pound lean boneless sirloin steak
2   teaspoons dark sesame oil, divided
1   bunch green onions, sliced into
        1" pieces
2   cups prepackaged coleslaw

2   (3-ounce) packages beef-flavored
        ramen noodle soup
1½ cups water
2   tablespoons soy sauce

1 Cut steak diagonally across grain into very thin slices. Heat 1 teaspoon oil in a large nonstick skillet over medium-high heat. Add steak and onions; stir-fry 1 minute. Remove steak mixture from pan; keep warm. Heat remaining 1 teaspoon oil until hot. Add slaw; stir-fry 30 seconds. Remove slaw from pan, and keep warm.

2 Remove noodles from packages; reserve 1 seasoning packet for another use. Add the water and remaining seasoning packet to pan; bring to a boil. Break noodles in half; add noodles to water mixture. Cook noodles 2 minutes or until most of the liquid is absorbed, stirring frequently. Stir in steak mixture, slaw, and soy sauce; cook until thoroughly heated.

" Even if you're running very, very late, you'll have time to make this quick stir-fry! "

Smothered Steak 'n' Gravy

6 servings

1   (10¾-ounce) can beefy mushroom
      soup, divided
1½ pounds ground chuck
1   large egg, beaten
½   cup fine, dry breadcrumbs
      (store-bought)
¼   cup finely chopped onion
⅛   teaspoon pepper

¼   cup water

1 Combine ¼ cup soup, ground chuck, and next 4 ingredients, mixing well. Divide meat mixture evenly into 6 portions. Shape each portion into a ½"-thick patty.

2 Cook patties in a large nonstick skillet over medium-high heat 3 to 4 minutes on each side or until browned.

3 Combine remaining soup and water, stirring well. Pour soup mixture over patties; cover, reduce heat, and simmer 20 minutes or until done. Serve immediately.

" I like to serve these savory patties with plenty of mashed potatoes or hot cooked rice to soak up every bit of the mushroom gravy. These patties are comfort food at its best! "

Bubble Pizza

8 servings

1½ pounds ground chuck

1   (14-ounce) jar pizza sauce
2   (12-ounce) cans refrigerated
     buttermilk biscuits, quartered

2   cups (8 ounces) shredded
     mozzarella cheese
2   cups (8 ounces) shredded sharp
     Cheddar cheese

1 Preheat the oven to 350°. Brown ground chuck in a large skillet, stirring until it crumbles and is no longer pink; drain in a colander, discarding drippings. Return meat to skillet.

2 Add pizza sauce, and stir well. Stir in quartered biscuits. Spoon mixture into a lightly greased 9" x 13" baking dish. Bake at 350° for 25 minutes.

3 Sprinkle with cheeses; bake 10 minutes. Let stand 5 minutes before serving.

Billowy Biscuit Topping

Cutting each biscuit into fourths creates the "bubbly-looking" topping on this cheesy deep-dish pizza casserole.

10-Minute Stroganoff

6 servings

1½ pounds ground beef

1   (8-ounce) package presliced fresh
     mushrooms
1   large onion, thinly sliced

1   (16-ounce) carton sour cream
1   (10¾-ounce) can cream of
     mushroom soup, undiluted
Garlic salt and pepper to taste (optional)

1 Brown ground beef in a large skillet, stirring until it crumbles and is no longer pink; drain in a colander, discarding drippings. Set ground beef aside.

2 Add mushrooms and onion to skillet, and cook over medium-high heat, stirring constantly, 5 minutes or until tender.

3 Add ground beef, sour cream, and soup; cook over medium heat 5 minutes or until thoroughly heated, stirring occasionally. If desired, stir in garlic salt and pepper to taste. Serve immediately over hot cooked egg noodles.

" This is my kind of meal—fast and just a pot and a pan to wash. No problem for the cook or the dishwasher!"

Surprise Burgers

6 servings

1½ cups (6 ounces) shredded Monterey Jack cheese
⅓ cup chopped ripe olives
⅛ teaspoon hot sauce

1¾ pounds ground chuck
¼ cup chopped onion (optional)
1 teaspoon salt
½ teaspoon pepper

1 Preheat the grill. Combine first 3 ingredients; stir well. Shape cheese mixture into 6 balls. Set aside.

2 Combine ground chuck and next 3 ingredients in a large bowl; stir well, and shape into 12 patties. Place a cheese ball in center of 6 patties; flatten cheese balls slightly. Top each with a second patty, pressing edges to seal. Grill, covered, over medium-high heat (350° to 400°) 5 to 6 minutes on each side or until done.

" Bite into these burgers and . . . surprise! Inside 'em are pockets of Monterey Jack cheese and ripe olives. "

Skillet Sombrero Pie

4 servings

1   pound ground round

1   (10-ounce) package frozen whole
     kernel corn, thawed
1   (14.5-ounce) can diced tomatoes
     with green pepper, celery, and
     onions, undrained
1   (8-ounce) can tomato sauce
1   (1¼-ounce) envelope taco
     seasoning mix

1   cup (4 ounces) shredded Cheddar
     cheese
1   (10½-ounce) package corn chips

1 Brown ground round in a large skillet, stirring until it crumbles and is no longer pink. Drain in a colander, discarding drippings.

2 Return meat to skillet. Add corn and next 3 ingredients; bring to a boil. Reduce heat; simmer, uncovered, 20 minutes, stirring occasionally.

3 Sprinkle with cheese; cook until cheese melts. Arrange chips around edge. Serve immediately.

No dinner dilemma here! This supper cooks all in one skillet. When it's done, scatter crunchy corn chips around the edge of the beef mixture to form the "brim" of this sombrero pie. If you can't find the canned tomatoes with vegetables, no problem. Just use plain diced tomatoes and throw in 1 tablespoon minced fresh onion!

Mighty Meatball Sandwiches

(pictured on page 38)
4 servings

1	pound ground round
3	tablespoons fine, dry breadcrumbs (store-bought)
⅓	cup chopped fresh mushrooms
2	tablespoons grated Parmesan cheese
1	large egg, lightly beaten
½	teaspoon ground nutmeg (optional)
1	teaspoon garlic salt
¼	teaspoon pepper

Store-bought spaghetti sauce

1 Preheat the oven to Broil. Combine first 8 ingredients in a large bowl; stir well. Shape meat mixture into 1" meatballs, and place on a rack in broiler pan coated with cooking spray.

2 Broil 5½" from heat for 16 minutes or until cooked through, turning occasionally. Serve topped with spaghetti sauce in a hoagie roll or over pasta.

❝Forget burgers! Try these hearty meatballs in a sandwich. They're so-o-o good!❞

Uptown Roast Beef Sandwiches

8 servings

1   pound thinly sliced cooked roast beef
3   avocados, peeled and cut into thin
      wedges
1   small purple onion, thinly sliced
1   cup vinaigrette dressing

2   (8.8-ounce) packages focaccia
Vegetable oil

4   (1-ounce) slices Monterey Jack
      cheese

1 Combine first 3 ingredients in a large heavy-duty, zip-top plastic bag. Pour vinaigrette dressing over beef mixture. Seal bag, and shake to coat. Marinate in refrigerator 8 hours, turning bag occasionally.

2 Preheat the oven to 375°. Place focaccia rounds on a large ungreased baking sheet; brush lightly with small amount of vegetable oil. Bake at 375° for 12 minutes or until lightly browned. Slice rounds in half horizontally.

3 Remove beef mixture from marinade, discarding marinade. Spoon beef mixture evenly onto bottom halves of focaccia rounds; top with cheese and remaining focaccia halves. Cut each sandwich into 4 wedges.

Focaccia for a Change
Focaccia is an Italian flatbread used as a sandwich bread for this tangy roast beef filling. If it's not available, use four hoagie rolls and cut each filled hoagie in half.

Melt-in-Your-Mouth Pork Chops

6 servings

1   tablespoon vegetable oil
6   (1"-thick) boneless center-cut loin
        pork chops
½   teaspoon salt
½   teaspoon pepper

12   pitted prunes
3   small onions, thinly sliced
½   cup water
2   tablespoons brown sugar
2   tablespoons cider vinegar

1 Heat vegetable oil in a large skillet over medium-high heat. Sprinkle pork chops with salt and pepper. Cook pork chops in hot oil 5 minutes on each side or until browned. Drain.

2 Add prunes and remaining ingredients to skillet. Cover, reduce heat to medium, and simmer, stirring occasionally, 30 minutes or until meat is tender.

" You'll love the sweet-and-sour taste sensation that the sugar and vinegar add to these oh-so-tender pork chops. "

Peachy Pork Picante

4 servings

1   pound pork tenderloin or other
     boneless pork, cubed

1   (1¼-ounce) envelope taco
     seasoning mix

1   tablespoon vegetable oil

¼   cup peach preserves

1   (8-ounce) jar mild salsa

1 Place pork in a large heavy-duty, zip-top plastic bag; add taco seasoning mix. Seal bag, and shake to coat pork.

2 Heat oil in a large skillet over medium-high heat. Add pork; cook, stirring constantly, until browned on all sides. Stir in preserves and salsa; cover, reduce heat, and simmer 15 minutes, stirring occasionally. Serve over warm cooked rice.

Pardner, taco seasoning and salsa add a kick to this pork. So, round up your family for this five-ingredient, 15-minute supper!

Sausage and Cheese Turnovers

10 turnovers

½ pound mild Italian sausage
¼ teaspoon dried Italian seasoning
1 (4-ounce) can mushroom stems and pieces, drained
1 cup (4 ounces) shredded mozzarella cheese

1 (10-ounce) can refrigerated flaky biscuits
1 large egg, beaten

1 tablespoon grated Parmesan cheese

1 Remove and discard casings from sausage. Brown sausage in a large skillet, stirring until it crumbles and is no longer pink. Drain in a colander, discarding drippings. Place sausage in a medium bowl. Stir in Italian seasoning, mushrooms, and mozzarella cheese; set aside.

2 Preheat the oven to 350°. Press each biscuit into a 5-inch circle. Spoon meat mixture evenly onto each circle. Moisten edges with beaten egg. Fold in half, and press edges together with a fork to seal.

3 Brush turnovers with beaten egg; sprinkle with Parmesan cheese. Place on a lightly greased baking sheet. Bake at 350° for 10 minutes or until golden.

❝ Toss the rolling pin and open a can of refrigerated biscuits. Stuff 'em with this sausage-cheese mixture, and presto—supper in a flash! ❞

Ham Steak Hawaiian

4 servings

½   cup packed brown sugar
¼   cup butter
¼   cup red wine vinegar

1   (½"-thick) slice fully cooked ham
     (about 1 pound)

1 Combine first 3 ingredients in a large skillet; cook over low heat, stirring constantly, until sugar dissolves and butter melts.

2 Add ham slice; cook over medium heat 5 minutes on each side or until thoroughly heated.

It's Your Choice
You can substitute white wine vinegar for red wine vinegar in this speedy entrée. Red and white wine vinegars both have a pleasantly pungent flavor that—teamed with the brown sugar—gives the sauce a sweet-and-sour twang!

Swiss-Ham Kabobs

6 servings

1 (20-ounce) can pineapple chunks in juice, drained with 2 tablespoons juice reserved

½ cup orange marmalade

1 tablespoon prepared mustard

¼ teaspoon ground cloves

1 pound cooked ham, cut into 1" cubes

8 ounces Swiss cheese, cut into 1" cubes

1 Combine reserved 2 tablespoons pineapple juice, the marmalade, mustard, and cloves; stir well with a wire whisk. Set mixture aside.

2 Preheat the grill. Alternately thread ham, cheese, ham, and pineapple chunks on 6 (12") skewers. (Cheese cubes must be between and touching ham to prevent rapid melting.) Place kabobs on grill rack. Brush with marmalade mixture. Grill, uncovered, over medium-high heat (350° to 400°) 3 to 4 minutes or until cheese is partially melted and ham is lightly browned, brushing often with marmalade mixture. Serve kabobs immediately.

Ham It Up!

Turn leftover ham into a feast as kabobs grilled with pineapple and Swiss cheese and topped with a tangy orange marmalade sauce.

Fish-in-Foil Packets

4 servings

4   (4-ounce) orange roughy, flounder, or sole fillets

4   green onions, thinly sliced
½   cup diced green bell pepper
¼   cup peeled and diced cucumber
1   tablespoon minced fresh ginger
1   tablespoon soy sauce
1   teaspoon olive oil

1 Preheat the oven to 450°. Cut 4 (15") squares of aluminum foil; place 1 fillet in center of each square.

2 Combine green onions and next 3 ingredients; sprinkle over fillets. Combine soy sauce and oil; drizzle over fillets. Fold foil over fillets; seal tightly. Bake at 450° for 10 to 12 minutes or until fish flakes easily when tested with a fork.

" Ginger and soy sauce give this simple fresh dish a touch of Thai flavoring. And cleanup's a cinch. Just crumble the foil, and toss it! "

Terrific Tuna Fettuccine

4 servings

8   ounces fettuccine, uncooked

1   cup sliced celery
¼   cup butter, melted
2   (8-ounce) packages cream cheese,
      cubed and softened
1⅓ cups milk
1   teaspoon onion salt
½   teaspoon pepper
2   (6⅛-ounce) cans solid white tuna,
      drained and flaked
1   cup grated Parmesan cheese

1 Cook pasta according to package directions, including salt; drain well. Set aside, and keep warm.

2 Cook celery in butter in a large skillet over medium-high heat, stirring constantly, until tender. Add cream cheese, milk, onion salt, and pepper; cook over medium heat until smooth, stirring occasionally. Stir in tuna and Parmesan cheese; cook until thoroughly heated, stirring occasionally.

3 Combine tuna mixture and pasta; toss well. Serve immediately.

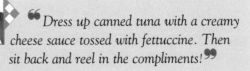

"Dress up canned tuna with a creamy cheese sauce tossed with fettuccine. Then sit back and reel in the compliments!"

Shrimp Marinara with Angel Hair Pasta

4 servings

1 pound unpeeled medium-size fresh shrimp

1 (9-ounce) package fresh angel hair pasta

1 tablespoon olive oil
2 cloves garlic, minced
1 (14-ounce) jar marinara sauce
1 tablespoon lime juice
1 teaspoon crushed red pepper

1 Peel shrimp, and devein, if desired.

2 Cook pasta according to package directions, including salt. Drain and set aside; cover to keep warm.

3 Heat oil in a large skillet over medium heat. Add garlic; cook 1 minute, stirring constantly. Add shrimp, and cook 3 to 5 minutes or until shrimp turn pink, stirring often. Add marinara sauce, lime juice, and red pepper; cook over medium heat until thoroughly heated. Serve over pasta.

Just Like Homemade
Shrimp, garlic, and crushed red pepper jazz up a jar of marinara for a sauce that mimics homemade.

Louisiana Baked Shrimp

(pictured on page 39)
4 servings

1½	pounds unpeeled medium-size fresh shrimp

⅓	cup butter
¼	cup dry red wine
2	tablespoons Worcestershire sauce
2	teaspoons chili powder
2	teaspoons freshly ground black pepper
2	teaspoons minced garlic
½	teaspoon salt
¼	teaspoon ground red pepper

1 Peel shrimp, and devein, if desired. Place shrimp in a single layer in an ungreased 9" x 13" baking dish.

2 Preheat the oven to 400°. Combine butter and next 7 ingredients in a saucepan. Cook over medium heat, stirring constantly, until butter melts. Pour over shrimp.

3 Bake, uncovered, at 400° for 8 minutes or until shrimp turn pink. Serve with a loaf of French or Italian bread.

Don't Miss A Drop

Serve these New Orleans-style baked shrimp with plenty of crusty bread to sop up the rich, buttery sauce.

Mexi-Cheesy Quesadillas

8 servings

4   cups (16 ounces) shredded
      Monterey Jack cheese
2   green onions, chopped
4   pickled jalapeño peppers, finely
      chopped
2   tablespoons minced fresh cilantro
1   teaspoon ground cumin

2   tablespoons butter, softened
8   (7") flour tortillas

1 Combine first 5 ingredients; stir well. Set aside.

2 Spread butter on 1 side of tortillas. Spoon cheese mixture evenly over unbuttered side of 4 tortillas; top with remaining 4 tortillas, buttered side up.

3 Cook quesadillas, one at a time, in a large skillet over medium-high heat 2 minutes on each side or until lightly browned. To serve, cut tortillas in half.

" Invite a few friends over for a Southwestern supper to start off the weekend. Serve these cheesy quesadillas with salsa and chilled beer, and let the fiesta begin!"

Eggplant Parmesan Express

6 servings

½ cup fine, dry breadcrumbs
(store-bought)
¾ cup grated Parmesan cheese
¼ cup mayonnaise
1 (1½-pound) eggplant, cut into
½" slices

1 (26-ounce) jar spaghetti sauce
4 (1½-ounce) slices mozzarella cheese

1 Preheat the oven to 425°. Combine breadcrumbs and Parmesan cheese. Thinly spread mayonnaise on each side of eggplant slices; dip both sides of eggplant in crumb mixture. Reserve remaining crumb mixture.

2 Place eggplant on an ungreased baking sheet, and bake at 425° for 15 minutes or until tender and lightly browned.

3 Place browned eggplant slices in a lightly greased 9" x 13" baking dish. Pour half of spaghetti sauce over slices; top with mozzarella cheese. Pour remaining spaghetti sauce over cheese; top with reserved crumb mixture. Bake at 375° for 15 minutes or until cheese melts.

Know Your Eggplant

Look for eggplants that are firm with smooth skin and no blemishes. They become bitter with age, so be sure to buy ones with bright green stem ends. Store in a cool, dry place and use within a few days of purchase.

Super Sideshow

"Complement your meal with any one, two, or three of these savory sides."

Sea Shell Mac 'n' Cheese

6 servings

1	(8-ounce) package shell macaroni
2	large eggs, separated
½	cup milk
½	cup finely chopped onions
2	tablespoons minced fresh parsley
¼	teaspoon salt
¼	teaspoon pepper
4	cups (16 ounces) shredded Cheddar cheese, divided

1 Cook macaroni according to package directions; drain well.

2 Preheat the oven to 350°. Combine macaroni, egg yolks, and next 5 ingredients in a large bowl; stir in 2 cups cheese.

3 Beat egg whites at high speed of an electric beater until stiff peaks form; fold into pasta mixture. Spoon into a greased 7" x 11" baking dish; sprinkle with remaining 2 cups cheese. Bake at 350° for 20 minutes.

" Kids and adults alike adore this old favorite with a new twist—seashell pasta! And little bits of onion and parsley add another new dimension. "

Lemon Vermicelli

4 servings

1/3 cup whipping cream
3 tablespoons butter

1 (7-ounce) package vermicelli
1/4 cup fresh lemon juice
1/3 cup freshly grated Parmesan cheese

1 Combine cream and butter in a small saucepan; cook over medium-low heat until butter melts. Set aside, and keep warm.

2 Cook vermicelli according to package directions; drain. Place in a large bowl, and toss with lemon juice; let stand 1 minute. Add cheese and warm cream mixture; toss. Serve immediately.

Add Zing!
A spritz of fresh lemon juice boosts the flavor of this rich, buttery, creamy pasta side dish.

Cumin Rice Timbales

6 servings

½ cup minced onion
1 teaspoon cumin seeds or ½
  teaspoon ground cumin
⅛ teaspoon crushed red pepper
2 tablespoons olive oil

1 cup converted rice, uncooked
1 (14½-ounce) can chicken broth
¼ cup water
¼ teaspoon salt
1 tablespoon minced fresh parsley

½ teaspoon cumin seeds, lightly toasted
  (optional)

1 Cook first 3 ingredients in oil in a large saucepan over medium-high heat, stirring constantly, until onion is tender.

2 Add rice; cook 1 minute, stirring constantly. Stir in chicken broth, water, and salt. Bring to a boil; cover, reduce heat, and simmer 20 minutes or until liquid is absorbed and rice is tender. Remove from heat, and stir in parsley. Cover and let stand 5 minutes.

3 Pack warm rice mixture into 6 (6-ounce) custard cups lightly coated with nonstick cooking spray. Immediately invert onto a serving platter. Sprinkle with toasted cumin seeds, if desired.

" Fancy schmancy is what I call these little rice molds. They look impressive on a dinner plate, but they're so easy to make. Just pack the cooked rice in a custard cup and invert it onto the serving plate. Voila! Toast cumin seeds to sprinkle on top, if you'd like. Just stir 'em in a dry skillet over medium heat 30 seconds or until toasted. "

Quick Hoppin' John

2 servings

3   slices bacon, chopped
½   cup chopped celery
⅓   cup chopped onion

1   cup water
1   (15-ounce) can black-eyed peas,
    undrained

1   cup quick long-grain rice, uncooked
½   teaspoon dried thyme

1 Cook bacon in a large saucepan until crisp, stirring often. Add celery and onion; cook, stirring constantly, until vegetables are tender.

2 Stir in water and peas; bring to a boil. Cover, reduce heat, and simmer 5 minutes.

3 Stir in rice and thyme. Remove from heat; cover and let stand 5 minutes or until liquid is absorbed and rice is tender.

" History has it that if you eat this old Southern favorite of rice and black-eyed peas on New Year's Day, you'll have good luck all year. I don't know about that, but I think we should eat 'em all year-round for good measure! "

Mexi Rice 'n' Cheese Casserole

8 servings

2   cups cooked rice
1   (8-ounce) container sour cream
1   (4.5-ounce) can chopped green
    chilies, undrained

2   cups (8 ounces) shredded Monterey
    Jack cheese

1 Preheat the oven to 350°. Combine first 3 ingredients in a large bowl. Spoon half of rice mixture into a lightly greased 7" x 11" baking dish.

2 Sprinkle half of cheese over rice mixture. Spoon remaining half of rice mixture over cheese, and sprinkle with remaining cheese. Bake, uncovered, at 350° for 25 minutes.

" So easy and so fine is what you'll say about this cheesy rice casserole that you can make from leftover rice. It goes great with any simple meat or poultry entrée or any Mexican main dish. "

Risotto in the Microwave

3½ cups

2 tablespoons butter
2 tablespoons olive oil
½ cup minced onion

1 cup Arborio rice or long- or whole-grain rice
3 cups chicken broth

½ cup freshly grated Parmesan cheese
¼ teaspoon pepper

1 Heat butter and oil in a microwave-safe 1½-quart glass or ceramic dish, uncovered, at HIGH 1 minute and 15 seconds to 2 minutes. Add onion; stir well. Cover and cook at HIGH 45 seconds to 1 minute.

2 Add rice, stirring well. Cover and cook at HIGH 3 to 4 minutes. Stir in chicken broth, and cook, uncovered, at HIGH 9 minutes. Stir well, and cook, uncovered, at HIGH 7 to 9 minutes. Remove from microwave oven, and let stand 5 minutes.

3 Stir in Parmesan cheese and pepper. Serve immediately.

> **"** I love the smooth and creamy texture of traditional risotto, but I'm too impatient to stand there and stir it the whole time. That's why I came up with this magic microwave method. You just give it a few quick stirs, and the microwave does the rest! True risotto is made with Arborio rice, but if you can't find it, substitute long- or whole-grain rice. **"**

Asparagus with Blue Cheese Vinaigrette

4 servings

1   pound fresh asparagus

2   tablespoons olive oil
2   teaspoons red wine vinegar
¼   cup crumbled blue cheese
2   tablespoons minced fresh chives
Ground white pepper

1 Snap off tough ends of asparagus; remove scales from stalks with a vegetable peeler, if desired. Add water to a medium skillet to depth of 1", and bring to a boil. Add asparagus in a single layer; cook 6 to 8 minutes or until crisp-tender. Drain asparagus, and arrange on a serving plate.

2 Combine oil and vinegar in a small bowl; stir well with a wire whisk. Add cheese and chives; stir well. Pour vinegar mixture over asparagus. Sprinkle with pepper.

Asparagus Tip!

For the tenderest asparagus, select long slender spears. Hold the spear with both hands and snap off the tough end where it seems to break naturally. What's left will cook up nice and tender!

Quick "Baked" Beans

4 servings

1 (21-ounce) can pork and beans
¼ cup ketchup
2 tablespoons brown sugar
1 tablespoon dried minced onion
½ teaspoon dry mustard

1 Combine all ingredients in a medium saucepan, stirring well. Bring to a boil; cover, reduce heat, and simmer 10 minutes, stirring occasionally.

" Who says you have to heat up the oven to have old-fashioned baked beans? Stir these up on the cooktop with a few simple seasonings, and your family will be all smiles! "

Easy Cheesy Broccoli Bake

6 servings

1½ pounds fresh broccoli

5   large eggs, lightly beaten
1   cup cottage cheese
2   tablespoons all-purpose flour
½   teaspoon salt
4   slices bacon, cooked and crumbled
½   cup (2 ounces) shredded Cheddar
      cheese

1 Preheat the oven to 350°. Remove and discard broccoli leaves and tough ends of stalks; cut broccoli into florets. Arrange broccoli in a steamer basket over boiling water. Cover and steam 3 minutes or until crisp-tender. Place broccoli in a lightly greased 7" x 11" baking dish.

2 Combine eggs and next 4 ingredients, stirring well; pour over broccoli. Bake at 350° for 20 minutes. Sprinkle with Cheddar cheese. Bake 5 minutes. Let stand 5 minutes before serving.

" Dotted with bits of smoky bacon, this cheesy broccoli dish is a new alternative to the typical broccoli casserole. It's special because it starts with fresh broccoli, which has so much texture and fresh appeal! "

Devilish Carrots

4 servings

1   pound carrots, peeled
½   cup butter, melted

2   tablespoons brown sugar
2   teaspoons dry mustard
2   drops hot sauce
½   teaspoon salt
Freshly ground pepper to taste

1 Cut carrots into 3" pieces, and quarter each piece. Cook carrots in butter in a large skillet over medium-high heat 5 minutes, stirring constantly.

2 Stir in brown sugar and remaining ingredients; cook 5 minutes or until tender. Serve immediately.

Hot sauce and dry mustard add the devilish flavor kick to these quick, easy carrots. If you want to cut corners, start with a pound of baby carrots. You don't have to peel 'em!

Lemon-Basil Green Beans

4 servings

¼ cup chopped fresh basil
2 tablespoons lemon juice
1 tablespoon olive oil
1 clove garlic, finely chopped
¼ teaspoon salt
⅛ teaspoon pepper

1 pound fresh green beans

1 Combine first 6 ingredients; cover and set aside while you prepare beans.

2 Wash beans; trim ends, and remove strings. Cover beans with water. Bring to a boil, and boil 6 to 8 minutes or until crisp-tender; drain well.

3 Pour marinade over beans. Cover and let stand at room temperature 45 minutes. Serve beans at room temperature.

Just Snip It!
To quickly chop fresh leafy herbs, such as basil, for this recipe, pack the herbs in a measuring cup, and snip them into little pieces with kitchen shears.

Peas to Perfection

4 servings

1   medium onion, chopped
3   tablespoons butter, melted

1   (10-ounce) package frozen sweet
     green peas
3   tablespoons chopped fresh cilantro
2   tablespoons minced fresh ginger
1   tablespoon ground cumin
¼   teaspoon salt

1 Cook onion in butter in a large skillet over medium-high heat, stirring constantly, until tender.

2 Add peas and remaining ingredients. Cover and cook over medium heat 4 to 5 minutes or until peas are tender, stirring often.

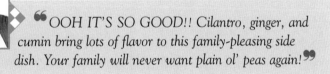

"OOH IT'S SO GOOD!! Cilantro, ginger, and cumin bring lots of flavor to this family-pleasing side dish. Your family will never want plain ol' peas again!"

Spiced Pickled Peaches

4 servings

1 (29-ounce) can peach halves in heavy syrup, drained and syrup reserved
½ cup cider vinegar
¾ cup packed brown sugar
1 teaspoon whole allspice
1 teaspoon whole cloves

Lettuce leaves

1 Combine peach syrup, vinegar, and next 3 ingredients in a medium saucepan. Bring to a boil; boil 5 minutes. Add peaches; reduce heat, and simmer, uncovered, 5 minutes. Let cool completely. Cover and chill 8 hours. Drain, discarding spices.

2 Serve peaches on lettuce-lined salad plates.

Peachy Idea
Serve these peaches as a tangy side dish or on a bed of lettuce as a light salad.

Fruited Acorn Squash

(pictured on page 3)
4 servings

2 medium acorn squash (1¼ to 1½ pounds each)

¾ cup peeled, seeded, and chopped orange
3 tablespoons brown sugar
½ teaspoon ground cinnamon
1 (8-ounce) can crushed pineapple, drained

1 Preheat the oven to 350°. Pierce squash with a fork, and arrange on paper towels in microwave. Microwave at HIGH 9 to 10 minutes or until tender. Cut in half, and remove seeds.

2 Combine orange and remaining 3 ingredients; spoon evenly into squash halves. Bake, uncovered, at 350° for 15 minutes or until squash is tender.

No Rockin' and Rollin' Here!
To keep squash halves upright as they bake, trim the bottom of each half to sit flat.

Sugar Snaps with Sesame Vinaigrette

(pictured on facing page)
4 servings

¼   cup sesame seeds

1   small clove garlic, crushed
1   tablespoon fresh lemon juice
¼   teaspoon salt
¼   teaspoon pepper
1   tablespoon red wine vinegar
2   tablespoons olive oil
1   teaspoon dark sesame oil

1   pound fresh sugar snap peas,
       trimmed

1 Cook sesame seeds in a skillet over medium heat 3 minutes or until toasted; remove from skillet, and let cool.

2 Combine garlic and next 3 ingredients in a large bowl. Stir in vinegar and oils, stirring well with a wire whisk.

3 Cook peas in a saucepan in a small amount of boiling water 30 seconds or to desired degree of doneness. Rinse under cold water to stop the cooking process, and drain. Add peas and sesame seeds to garlic mixture; toss well to coat. Serve at room temperature, or cover and chill.

It's a Snap!
Sugar snaps not in season? Use frozen sugar snap peas that have been thawed on paper towels. There's no need to cook the frozen variety before continuing with the recipe.

Pear-Walnut Salad, page 123

Sesame Knots, page 141

Corn, Okra, and Tomatoes

(pictured on facing page)
6 servings

1	large onion, chopped
1	large green bell pepper, chopped
2	cloves garlic, minced
⅓	cup butter
2	cups chopped plum tomatoes
4	ears fresh corn, cut from cob
1	cup sliced fresh okra
1	teaspoon salt
½	teaspoon freshly ground pepper

1 Cook first 3 ingredients in butter in a skillet over medium-high heat, stirring constantly, until tender.

2 Add tomatoes; bring to a boil. Reduce heat, and simmer, uncovered, 15 minutes.

3 Add corn and remaining ingredients; bring to a boil. Reduce heat, and simmer 9 minutes or until corn is tender.

The Fresher, the Better!
Raid your garden or the corner market for this savory summer side dish that my family adores. And remember, the fresher, the better when you're making a veggie dish such as this. Vegetables lose flavor and nutrients when they sit in the fridge!

Tomato Pie

6 servings

½ (15-ounce) package refrigerated
   piecrusts

2 large tomatoes, sliced
½ teaspoon dried basil
½ teaspoon dried chives
½ teaspoon pepper
½ cup mayonnaise
1 cup (4 ounces) shredded sharp
   Cheddar cheese

1 Preheat the oven to 450°. Fit piecrust into a 9" pie plate according to package directions; fold edges under, and crimp. Prick bottom and sides of crust with a fork. Bake at 450° for 9 minutes. Reduce oven temperature to 350°.

2 Arrange tomato slices in crust. Combine basil, chives, and pepper; sprinkle over tomatoes. Spread with mayonnaise; sprinkle with cheese.

3 Bake, uncovered, at 350° for 20 minutes or until cheese melts and pie is thoroughly heated. Let stand 10 minutes before slicing. Serve warm or let cool on a wire rack.

Dinner's Easy as Pie!

Sliced fresh tomatoes take on new meaning in this easy tomato pie. It bakes 20 minutes—long enough to grill some boneless chicken breasts or pork chops to serve alongside.

Rosemary Roasted Potatoes

4 servings

2 pounds small red potatoes,
  unpeeled and quartered
2 cloves garlic, minced
1 tablespoon chopped fresh rosemary
1 tablespoon olive oil
¼ teaspoon salt
⅛ teaspoon pepper

1 Preheat the oven to 450°. Combine all ingredients in a large bowl or large heavy-duty, zip-top plastic bag. Stir mixture in bowl or seal bag, and shake well to coat.

2 Arrange potatoes in a well-greased 9" x 13" baking dish. Bake, uncovered, at 450° for 35 to 40 minutes or until potatoes are tender.

Less work than mashed potatoes and more flavorful than plain rice, these crisp roasted potatoes will become a favorite dinner partner at your house, too, I betcha!

Skillet Potatoes

4 servings

½   cup vegetable oil
3   large red potatoes, peeled and cut
      into 1½" chunks

1   small onion, chopped
Salt and pepper to taste

1 Heat oil in a 9" or 10" cast-iron or nonstick skillet over medium-high heat. Fry potato chunks in hot oil 12 minutes, turning often.

2 Add onion, and cook 5 more minutes. Remove mixture to a serving bowl, using a slotted spoon. Sprinkle with salt and pepper.

" Save time and leave the skins on the potatoes, if you'd like. The potatoes will fry up crispy brown, especially if you use a cast-iron skillet. You'll get the benefit of great taste and a dose of iron to boot!"

Soup and Salad Bar

❝Mosey up to my bar for a fabulous array of sensational soups and salads.❞

Frosty Cantaloupe Soup

8½ cups

1	medium-size ripe cantaloupe, cubed
3	cups vanilla ice cream, softened
¼	cup honey
½	(6-ounce) can frozen orange juice concentrate

1½ cups ginger ale, chilled
Garnish: fresh mint leaves

1 Process first 4 ingredients, in batches, in a food processor until smooth; transfer to a large pitcher or serving bowl. Cover mixture, and chill at least 30 minutes.

2 Gently stir in ginger ale just before serving. Garnish individual servings, if desired. Serve immediately.

Take out your prettiest bowls for this sweet dessert soup, and float fresh mint leaves on top of each serving. You can make the soup ahead, but wait till the last minute to stir in the ginger ale to keep it fresh and bubbly!

Chinese Egg Drop Soup

4 cups

2   (14½-ounce) cans chicken broth
2   large eggs, beaten

1   cup sliced fresh mushrooms
¼   cup diced water chestnuts
¼   cup coarsely chopped fresh snow
       pea pods
1   tablespoon soy sauce
½   cup bean sprouts (optional)

1 Bring chicken broth to a boil in a large saucepan. Gradually drizzle beaten eggs into soup, stirring well.

2 Stir in mushrooms and remaining ingredients, including bean sprouts, if desired; reduce heat to low, and cook until thoroughly heated.

> " *Here's my quick version of the trademark soup many Chinese restaurants serve. The trick to getting the lacy strands of egg is to drizzle the beaten eggs into the hot broth in a thin stream, stirring the soup constantly.* "

Cream of Pimiento Soup

6½ cups

2 cups water
2 chicken bouillon cubes
2 (7-ounce) jars diced pimientos, drained

⅓ cup butter
¼ cup all-purpose flour
3 cups half-and-half
Salt and freshly ground pepper to taste

Garnishes: sour cream, fresh dill sprigs

66 I serve this delicately flavored soup hot in the winter and chilled in the summer. It makes a fancy schmancy appetizer course when company's coming! 99

1 Bring first 3 ingredients to a boil in a medium saucepan, stirring frequently to dissolve bouillon cubes. Remove from heat, and let cool slightly. Pour pimiento mixture into container of an electric blender; process until smooth, stopping once to scrape down sides.

2 Melt butter in a large heavy saucepan over low heat. Add flour, stirring until smooth. Cook 1 minute, stirring constantly. Gradually add half-and-half; cook over medium heat, stirring constantly, until mixture is thickened and bubbly. Reduce heat to low; add pimiento mixture and salt and pepper to taste. Cook until heated, stirring occasionally.

3 Serve immediately, or cover and chill. Garnish individual servings, if desired.

Fresh Tomato Soup

3 cups

2 cups peeled, diced ripe tomato
3 tablespoons butter
2 tablespoons all-purpose flour
1 teaspoon salt
1/8 teaspoon pepper

1 cup half-and-half
1/4 to 1/2 cup dry white wine or no-salt-added chicken broth

1 Combine tomato and butter in a large saucepan. Bring to a boil; reduce heat, and simmer, uncovered, 5 minutes. Process mixture in container of an electric blender until smooth, stopping once to scrape down sides. Add flour, salt, and pepper; process until blended.

2 Return mixture to saucepan; bring to a boil. Reduce heat, and simmer 2 to 3 minutes, stirring constantly. Add half-and-half; cook until slightly thickened, stirring often. Stir in wine, and bring just to a boil.

No Substitutes!

You'll want to use fresh-from-the-vine tomatoes in this refreshing soup. Once they're picked, tomatoes start to lose flavor, especially if you store them in the fridge. Keep 'em on the counter and use 'em soon or lose 'em!

Easy Corn and Crabmeat Soup

6 cups

¼ cup butter
¼ cup all-purpose flour
2 cups water

2 cups half-and-half
1 pound fresh lump crabmeat, drained
1 (11-ounce) can whole kernel corn, drained
2 tablespoons chicken bouillon granules
¾ teaspoon garlic salt
¼ teaspoon pepper

1 Melt butter in a large heavy saucepan over low heat; add flour, stirring until smooth. Cook 1 minute, stirring constantly. Gradually add water; cook over medium heat, stirring constantly, until thickened.

2 Stir in half-and-half and remaining ingredients; cover, reduce heat, and simmer 20 minutes.

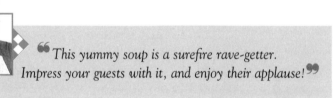

This yummy soup is a surefire rave-getter. Impress your guests with it, and enjoy their applause!

Mexican Chicken Soup

7 cups

2   (14½-ounce) cans chicken broth
1   medium onion, thinly sliced and
      separated into rings
2   large red or green bell peppers, cut
      into very thin strips
⅔   cup thinly sliced carrot
⅔   cup thinly sliced celery
¾   teaspoon seasoned salt
1   cup shredded cooked chicken breast
2   to 3 tablespoons chopped fresh
      cilantro
2   tablespoons fresh lime juice

4   (6-inch) corn tortillas
2   tablespoons vegetable oil

1 Combine first 6 ingredients in a large saucepan; bring to a boil. Cover, reduce heat, and simmer 10 minutes. Stir in chicken, cilantro, and lime juice; cook until thoroughly heated.

2 Meanwhile, cut each tortilla into thin strips. Heat oil in a large skillet until hot. Add tortilla strips, and fry 3 to 4 minutes or until crisp. Drain tortilla strips on paper towels.

3 Serve immediately. Top each serving with tortilla strips.

My south-of-the-border soup comes complete with its own crackers—crunchy strips of fried corn tortillas. The soup cooks in 10 minutes—just enough time to fry up the crispy strips!

Beef-Tortellini Soup

11½ cups

1   pound ground beef

3   cups water
1   (28-ounce) can tomato puree
1   (10½-ounce) can French onion soup,
        undiluted
1   (9-ounce) package frozen cut green
        beans
1   (9-ounce) package refrigerated
        cheese-filled tortellini
1   medium zucchini, chopped

1 Brown ground beef in a large Dutch oven, stirring until it crumbles and is no longer pink; drain in a colander, discarding drippings. Return meat to Dutch oven.

2 Stir in water and next 4 ingredients. Bring to a boil; cover, reduce heat, and simmer 10 minutes. Add zucchini, and cook, uncovered, 15 minutes.

No Limits
For a change of pace, try fresh ground turkey instead of beef, and replace the zucchini with yellow squash.

Super-Easy Chili

6 cups

1   pound ground chuck
1   small onion, chopped
1   teaspoon minced garlic

1   (16-ounce) can chili hot beans,
      undrained
1   (6-ounce) can tomato paste
1½ cups water
1   tablespoon chili powder
1   teaspoon salt

1 Combine first 3 ingredients in a Dutch oven; cook until beef is browned, stirring until it crumbles and is no longer pink. Drain in a colander, discarding drippings. Return meat to Dutch oven.

2 Add beans and remaining ingredients to Dutch oven; cover, reduce heat, and simmer 15 minutes, stirring mixture occasionally.

" Talk about hearty—this chili's it! Chock-full of ground chuck and hot beans, it's so easy to make. Serve it with your favorite cornbread recipe tonight! "

Cranberry-Eggnog Gelatin Salad

8 servings

1   (8-ounce) can crushed pineapple, undrained
1   envelope unflavored gelatin
1½ cups eggnog

1½ cups cranberry juice drink
1   (3-ounce) package raspberry-flavored gelatin

1   (12-ounce) container cranberry-orange relish
½   cup finely chopped celery

1 Place pineapple in a saucepan. Sprinkle unflavored gelatin over pineapple; let stand 1 minute. Cook over low heat, stirring 2 minutes or until gelatin dissolves; cool. Stir in eggnog. Pour into an ungreased 7" x 11" baking dish. Cover and chill until firm.

2 Pour juice drink into a small saucepan; bring to a boil. Place raspberry gelatin in a bowl; add juice drink, stirring 2 minutes or until gelatin dissolves. Chill until consistency of unbeaten egg white.

3 Fold in relish and chopped celery. Carefully spoon over eggnog mixture. Chill until firm. Cut into squares.

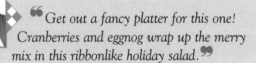

Get out a fancy platter for this one! Cranberries and eggnog wrap up the merry mix in this ribbonlike holiday salad.

Pear-Walnut Salad

(pictured on page 106)
5 servings

4   cups tightly packed torn mixed
     salad greens
1½ cups walnut halves, toasted
2   ripe red pears, cored and sliced
2   ounces crumbled blue cheese
Tangy-Sweet Dressing

1 Combine first 4 ingredients in a large bowl; toss gently. Pour Tangy-Sweet Dressing over salad mixture just before serving; toss.

Tangy-Sweet Dressing

½   cup olive oil
3   tablespoons white vinegar
¼   cup sugar
½   teaspoon celery seeds
¼   teaspoon salt

Combine all ingredients in a small jar; cover tightly, and shake vigorously.
Yield: 1 cup

Opposites Attract!
This autumn salad is proof positive that opposites attract. The natural sweetness of the ripe, tender pears plays off the tang of the blue cheese perfectly. And Tangy-Sweet Dressing marries the flavors!

Raspberry Green Salad

8 servings

½   cup olive oil
¼   cup raspberry vinegar
2   tablespoons honey
½   teaspoon pepper
¼   teaspoon salt
1   clove garlic, minced

1   (6½-ounce) package mixed baby
       salad greens
2   cups fresh raspberries

1 Combine first 6 ingredients in a small jar. Cover tightly, and shake vigorously.

2 Pour dressing over salad greens; toss gently to coat. Top with raspberries.

" If you don't want to buy a package of baby salad greens, use 8 cups of any mixture of torn lettuce that you like. Just toss the greens with the raspberry vinaigrette, and sprinkle fresh raspberries over the top. You'll think you're in a fancy restaurant!"

Asparagus and Goat Cheese Salad

6 servings

1 pound fresh asparagus

2 tablespoons cider vinegar
½ teaspoon salt
¼ teaspoon pepper
⅓ cup vegetable oil

1 large head Boston lettuce, torn
2 ounces goat cheese

1 Snap off tough ends of asparagus. Remove scales from stalks with a vegetable peeler, if desired. Cook asparagus in a small amount of boiling water 3 minutes or until crisp-tender. Drain well, and set aside.

2 Combine vinegar, salt, and pepper in a small bowl; add oil in a thin stream, whisking until blended. Pour dressing over asparagus; toss gently to coat.

3 To serve, divide lettuce evenly among 6 individual salad plates. Spoon asparagus over lettuce; crumble cheese evenly over asparagus.

Rite of Spring

Spring's the season when delicate, pencil-thin asparagus are at their peak. Before you cook 'em, snap 'em! That is, hold a spear in one hand and snap off the tough end with the other hand; what's left will cook up oh-so-tender!

Three-Bean and Cilantro Salad

6 servings

1   (16-ounce) can kidney beans,
        drained
1   (15-ounce) can black beans, drained
1   (15-ounce) can chickpeas, drained
½   cup chopped fresh cilantro
⅓   cup olive oil
¼   cup balsamic vinegar

1 Combine all ingredients in a large bowl; toss well. Cover and chill at least 3 hours, stirring occasionally.

Easy as 1, 2, 3

Three cans of beans and three marinade ingredients—can't get much simpler than that! Just stash the salad in the fridge till you're ready for it.

Black-Eyed Pea Salad

6 servings

2 (15½-ounce) cans black-eyed peas,
    rinsed and drained
1 ripe avocado, peeled and chopped
1 medium tomato, chopped
1 medium onion, chopped
½ cup sweet-and-spicy French salad
    dressing

1 Combine all ingredients in a large bowl; toss well. Cover and chill 8 hours.

Chop, Chop!
Chopped fresh avocado, tomato, and onion dress up canned black-eyed peas in this super make-ahead salad.

127

Spinach-Strawberry Salad with Pecans

6 servings

1   (10-ounce) package fresh spinach,
      torn
1   cup strawberries, halved
1   cup pecan halves, toasted
Poppy seed dressing (store-bought)

1 Combine first 3 ingredients in a large bowl; drizzle with poppy seed dressing. Serve immediately.

" Toasted pecans and fresh berries turn spinach into something special. No one will know you used a bottled dressing—unless you tell 'em! "

Tomato-Basil Rice

4 servings

3   cups cooked rice
1   cup coarsely chopped tomato
2   tablespoons coarsely chopped fresh
      basil
½   teaspoon salt

1 Combine all ingredients in a medium bowl, tossing gently. Serve immediately, or cover and chill up to 8 hours.

Rice is Nice!
This easy dish is so obliging! You can serve it cold as a salad or warm as a side dish. Drizzle it with balsamic vinegar for even more flavor.

Presto Pasta Salad

4 servings

8   ounces dried rotini pasta, uncooked

1½ cups broccoli florets
1   cup sliced fresh mushrooms
1   large red bell pepper, seeded and
     cut into 1" pieces
1   (8-ounce) bottle Caesar salad dressing

1 Cook pasta according to package directions, including salt; drain. Rinse with cold water; drain and place in a large bowl.

2 Add broccoli and remaining 3 ingredients to pasta; toss well. Cover and chill, if desired.

" I just love this salad because I just love rotini pasta—you know, the kind that looks like little corkscrews. It stands up nicely to the crunchy veggies in this recipe. "

Sweet 'n' Tangy Salad Dressing

2 cups

½ cup sugar
½ cup white vinegar
½ cup vegetable oil
½ cup hot ketchup
1 tablespoon chopped fresh chives
1 clove garlic, halved
¼ teaspoon celery salt
¼ teaspoon salt
⅛ teaspoon pepper

1 Combine all ingredients in a medium bowl; beat with a wire whisk until blended. Cover and chill at least 8 hours. Remove and discard garlic. Store dressing in an airtight container in refrigerator up to 2 weeks. Serve dressing over salad greens.

A Tangy-Sweet Temptation
Sugar gives this dressing its sweetness, and hot ketchup its pizzazz! If you don't have hot ketchup, splash a little hot sauce into regular ketchup to your liking!

Home-Style Ranch Dressing

2 cups

1   cup buttermilk
1   cup mayonnaise
1   tablespoon dried parsley flakes
2   teaspoons dried minced onion
¼   teaspoon salt
⅛   teaspoon garlic powder

1 Combine all ingredients in a medium bowl; stir well. Cover and chill thoroughly. Serve dressing over salad greens.

" If you're watching your waistline, simply substitute low-fat buttermilk and mayonnaise for regular—everyone will still pony up for that great ranch flavor! "

Breadshoppe Bounty

❝Homemade goodness in half the time is what you'll discover when you bake from this bountiful collection of oh-so-easy breads.❞

Cheese-Garlic Biscuits

10 biscuits

2 cups biscuit mix
⅔ cup milk
½ cup (2 ounces) shredded sharp
    Cheddar cheese

¼ cup butter, melted
¼ teaspoon garlic powder

1 Preheat the oven to 350°. Combine first 3 ingredients in a medium bowl; beat with a wooden spoon until blended.

2 Drop dough by heaping tablespoonfuls onto an ungreased baking sheet. Bake at 350° for 12 to 13 minutes or until golden.

3 Combine butter and garlic powder; brush over tops of biscuits. Serve immediately.

No kneading or cutting required when you make these easy drop biscuits— you're gonna love 'em!

Cheater's Beaten Biscuits

2 dozen

2 cups all-purpose flour
1 teaspoon salt
½ cup cold butter, cut into small
  pieces

⅓ cup ice water

1 Preheat the oven to 400°. Position knife blade in food processor bowl; add flour and salt. Process 5 seconds; add butter, and process 10 seconds or until mixture is crumbly.

2 Pour water through food chute with processor running; process until mixture forms a ball. Turn dough out onto a lightly floured surface. Roll dough into a ⅛"-thick rectangle. Fold dough in half lengthwise; cut with a 1" biscuit cutter. Place on an ungreased baking sheet. Prick top of each biscuit with a fork 3 times. Bake at 400° for 20 minutes or until lightly browned.

"Old-timers beat their biscuit dough 30 to 45 minutes with a rolling pin to achieve the characteristic texture of these crisp little biscuits. But I traded in my rolling pin for a food processor, and the job's done in a jiffy! These biscuits with flaky layers split naturally to form perfect pockets for your choice of partners."

Dried Cherry Scones

10 scones

½   cup sugar, divided
2¾ cups biscuit mix
¼   cup butter, cut into small pieces

½   cup dried sweet cherries
1   (8-ounce) container cherry vanilla
    fat-free yogurt

Dried cherries and a container of cherry yogurt turn biscuit mix into a fancy-schmancy breakfast treat. And you can forget the rolling pin for these sweet little scones. Just pat the dough into a circle, and cut it into wedges.

1 Preheat the oven to 400°. Reserve 1 tablespoon sugar to sprinkle over top of scones; set aside. Combine the remaining sugar and biscuit mix in a bowl; stir well. Cut in butter with a pastry blender or 2 knives until mixture is crumbly.

2 Add cherries and yogurt, stirring just until moist (dough will be sticky). Turn dough out onto a lightly floured surface. Knead with floured hands 4 or 5 times. Pat dough into a 9" circle on a lightly greased baking sheet. Cut into 10 wedges with a lightly floured knife, cutting into, but not through, dough.

3 Sprinkle reserved 1 tablespoon sugar over dough. Bake at 400° for 18 minutes or until golden.

Merry Berry Muffins

1 dozen

2¼ cups biscuit mix
⅓ to ½ cup sugar

1 large egg, lightly beaten
1 cup buttermilk
¼ cup butter, melted
1 cup fresh whole berries (see box below)

1 tablespoon sugar

1 Preheat the oven to 425°. Combine biscuit mix and ⅓ to ½ cup sugar (see box below) in a large bowl; make a well in center of mixture.

2 Combine egg, buttermilk, and butter in a small bowl; add to dry ingredients, stirring just until moist. Stir in berries.

3 Spoon batter into greased muffin pan, filling three-fourths full. Sprinkle 1 tablespoon sugar evenly over batter. Bake at 425° for 18 minutes. Remove from pan immediately.

"These muffins are merry 'cause you pick the berry! Your choice of berry, that is! I recommend fresh raspberries, blueberries, or blackberries. If you use strawberries, be sure to quarter 'em. And you decide on the amount of sugar to add depending on the sweetness of the berries and how you like your muffins—tart or sweet!"

Surprise 'Nana Muffins

½ dozen

1 (6.4-ounce) package banana nut
  muffin mix
⅓ cup buttermilk
1 large egg, lightly beaten

¼ cup fig preserves or strawberry jam
2 tablespoons chopped dates or
  raisins

1 Preheat the oven to 400°. Combine first 3 ingredients in a medium bowl; stir just until moist. Spoon about 1 tablespoon batter into each of 6 lightly greased muffin cups, spreading batter to cover bottom of cups.

2 Spoon 2 teaspoons fig preserves and 1 teaspoon dates into center of each cup; divide remaining batter evenly among muffin cups to cover fruit. Bake at 400° for 15 minutes. Remove from pan immediately.

"What's the surprise? Little chunks of dried fruit and preserves hide in the middle of these banana muffins. And there's no fuss mashing bananas—just start with a packaged muffin mix!"

Onion Popovers

8 popovers

1 cup all-purpose flour
¾ teaspoon onion salt
1 teaspoon dried parsley flakes
1 cup milk
2 large eggs, lightly beaten

1 Preheat the oven to 450°. Combine first 3 ingredients in a medium bowl; make a well in center of mixture. Combine milk and eggs in a small bowl; add to dry ingredients, stirring until mixture is almost smooth. Spoon batter into 8 greased 6-ounce ovenproof custard cups or muffin cups.

2 Bake at 450° for 20 minutes. Reduce heat to 350°, and bake 15 more minutes. Remove from custard cups immediately.

"I love to watch these tasty little rolls puff up in the oven! They'll puff the highest if you bake 'em in the custard cups, but muffin pans work fine, too. Boy, are these yummy!"

Butter-Me-Up Breadsticks

32 breadsticks

½ (32-ounce) package frozen bread
    dough, thawed

1 cup grated Parmesan cheese
1½ teaspoons dried Italian seasoning
½ cup butter, melted

1 Preheat the oven to 450°. Divide bread dough into 8 portions; divide each portion into 4 pieces. Roll each piece into a 4" strip.

2 Combine cheese and Italian seasoning on a plate; dip strips into melted butter, and roll strips in cheese mixture. Place strips on greased baking sheets. Bake at 450° for 6 to 7 minutes or until lightly browned.

❝My breadsticks are so-o-o easy! I simply start with a package of frozen bread dough and enhance it with a bit of this and that—that's all there is to it!❞

Sesame Knots

(pictured on page 107)
8 servings

1   (11-ounce) can refrigerated
        breadsticks

2   tablespoons butter, melted
1   teaspoon sesame seeds

1 Preheat the oven to 350°. Separate dough, and loosely tie each piece of dough into a knot; place 1" apart on an ungreased baking sheet.

2 Brush knots with melted butter, and sprinkle with sesame seeds. Bake at 350° for 15 minutes or until golden.

" These fancy rolls won't leave you fit to be tied—promise! With only three ingredients, they're super easy to make, and they look great! "

Quick 'n' Cheesy Bacon Swirls

16 servings

1   (8-ounce) can refrigerated crescent dinner rolls

5   slices bacon, cooked and crumbled
1   (3-ounce) package cream cheese, softened
2   tablespoons finely chopped onion
1   teaspoon milk

Grated Parmesan cheese

1 Preheat the oven to 375°. Separate refrigerated dough into 4 rectangles; gently press perforations to seal.

2 Combine bacon and next 3 ingredients in a small bowl, stirring well. Spread bacon mixture evenly over rectangles. Roll up rectangles, starting at long side; pinch seams to seal.

3 Cut each roll into 8 slices; place slices, cut side down, on ungreased baking sheets. Sprinkle with Parmesan cheese. Bake at 375° for 12 to 15 minutes or until golden. Serve warm.

Say Cheese!
Forget the crackers when you serve up canned tomato soup. Whip up these cheesy little swirls to serve alongside, and your family will think supper's extra special!

Fine Wine French Bread

1 loaf

1 (16-ounce) loaf French bread
½ cup butter, softened
½ cup freshly grated Parmesan cheese
¼ cup dry red wine
2 teaspoons dried Italian seasoning
¼ teaspoon garlic powder

1 Preheat the oven to 400°. Cut bread into 1" slices, cutting to, but not through, bottom of loaf; place loaf on an ungreased baking sheet. Combine butter and remaining 4 ingredients in a small bowl; stir well (wine will not blend completely).

2 Spread mixture evenly on each side of bread slices. Bake loaf, uncovered, at 400° for 10 minutes.

It's No Joke!

This fancy French bread makes a perfect partner for a steak! A little red wine flavors the garlic butter just right for a meat 'n' potatoes-lovin' guy like me! And you can pour up the rest of the wine for dinner!

Green Chilie Cornbread

15 servings

2   (7½-ounce) packages corn muffin
     mix
1   (8½-ounce) can cream-style corn
1   (4.5-ounce) can chopped green
     chilies, drained
1   cup (4 ounces) shredded Cheddar
     cheese
½   cup plain yogurt
¼   cup milk
2   large eggs, lightly beaten

1 Preheat the oven to 450°. Combine all ingredients in a large bowl, stirring just until moistened.

2 Pour batter into a lightly greased 9" x 13" pan. Bake at 450° for 20 minutes or until golden. Cut into squares to serve.

"M-m-m! Cream-style corn provides a slight sweetness to this pan of cheesy goodness!"

Italian Pull-Apart Loaf

8 servings

1 (16-ounce) loaf unsliced Italian
bread

¾ cup butter, softened
½ cup (about 2 ounces) coarsely
chopped prosciutto
⅓ cup grated Parmesan cheese
2 teaspoons dried basil
½ teaspoon freshly ground pepper

1 Preheat the oven to 450°. Slice bread cutting to, but not through, bottom in a crisscross fashion, making a diamond pattern down the loaf of bread.

2 Combine butter and next 4 ingredients in a small bowl, stirring well. Spread butter mixture between bread slices. Place on an ungreased baking sheet. Bake, uncovered, at 450° for 5 minutes or until thoroughly heated. To serve, pull apart bread pieces.

" *Salty prosciutto (Italian ham) and butter dot every bite-size piece of this savory bread. Enjoy it with a crispy green salad.* "

Double Cheese-Topped French Bread

8 servings

1   (10-ounce) package frozen chopped spinach, thawed and well drained

½   teaspoon garlic powder

2   cups (8 ounces) shredded Cheddar cheese

2   cups (8 ounces) shredded mozzarella cheese

½   cup butter, melted

1   (16-ounce) loaf French bread, cut in half horizontally

1 Preheat the oven to 350°. Combine first 5 ingredients in a large bowl, and stir well.

2 Place bread halves on an ungreased baking sheet. Spread mixture evenly on bread halves. Bake, uncovered, at 350° for 15 minutes or until cheeses melt. Cut into slices to serve.

" What a delicious way to sneak a bit of green into your family's meal. This spinach-topped cheese bread is so good, everybody will be back for more!"

"Salad" Bread

1 (10") ring

½ cup chopped onion
½ cup chopped red or green bell
    pepper
½ cup chopped celery
½ cup butter, melted
3 (12-ounce) cans flaky biscuits
1 cup (4 ounces) shredded Cheddar
    cheese

1 Preheat the oven to 350°. Cook first 3 ingredients in melted butter in a large skillet until tender, stirring often. Cut biscuits into fourths. Dip biscuit pieces in vegetable mixture, coating with butter and vegetables. Place pieces in a lightly greased 10" Bundt pan; sprinkle with cheese.

2 Bake at 350° for 40 minutes or until golden. Cool in pan 10 minutes; invert onto a serving platter, and serve immediately.

" I've taken canned biscuits and laced 'em with bits of chopped veggies and shredded cheese for a pull-apart bread that's almost a meal in itself. "

Cranberry Sweet Rolls

1 dozen

1	(10-ounce) can refrigerated pizza crust dough
½	cup orange marmalade
⅔	cup dried cranberries
½	cup sifted powdered sugar
1½	teaspoons lemon juice
1	teaspoon hot water

1 Preheat the oven to 375°. Unroll pizza dough; pat into a 9" x 12" rectangle. Spread marmalade over dough, leaving a ½" border. Sprinkle cranberries over marmalade, pressing gently into dough. Beginning with a long side, roll up dough, jellyroll fashion; pinch seam to seal (do not seal ends of roll). Cut roll into 12 (1") slices (see box below). Place slices, cut sides up, in a lightly greased muffin pan.

2 Bake at 375° for 15 minutes or until golden. Remove rolls from pan, and place on a wire rack. Combine powdered sugar, lemon juice, and hot water in a small bowl, stirring until smooth. Drizzle over warm rolls.

Make a "Clean" Cut!

Wanna know how to cut this roll of dough into the neatest, cleanest slices? Dental floss! That's right! Simply place a 10" piece of floss under the dough, and cross the two strands over the top to cut a slice. Voila!

Beignets

21 beignets

1   (16-ounce) package frozen roll
        dough, thawed

Vegetable oil
Powdered sugar

1 Flatten and stretch each roll slightly.

2 Pour oil to depth of 2" into a Dutch oven; heat to 375°. Fry rolls, 4 at a time, in hot oil 1 to 2 minutes or until golden, turning often. Drain on paper towels. Sprinkle with powdered sugar; serve immediately.

❝ The recipe for this New Orleans favorite doesn't have to be complicated. These puffy little pillows are made with frozen roll dough—that's it! Just fry 'em up and sprinkle on the powdered sugar. And don't forget the café au lait!❞

Honey-Almond French Braid

8 servings

1   (11-ounce) can refrigerated French
    bread dough
2   tablespoons honey
½   teaspoon water
⅛   teaspoon ground ginger

2   tablespoons sliced almonds

1 Preheat the oven to 350°. Unroll dough; cut into 3 equal pieces. Shape each portion into a 10" rope. Place ropes on a baking sheet coated with nonstick cooking spray (do not stretch). Braid ropes together; pinch ends to seal. Combine honey, water, and ginger in a small bowl, stirring well. Brush braided dough with half of honey mixture.

2 Bake braid at 350° for 20 minutes. Remove from oven; brush with remaining honey mixture. Sprinkle with almonds. Bake 10 more minutes or until loaf sounds hollow when tapped. Remove from baking sheet immediately. Serve warm.

No "Knead" for Flour!
You won't even have to flour your counter to shape this homemade yeast bread. With refrigerated dough, you can roll and braid it right on the counter or a baking sheet!

Cinnamon Loaves

2 loaves

1 (18.25-ounce) package yellow cake mix
4 large eggs
¾ cup vegetable oil
¾ cup water
1 teaspoon vanilla extract

½ cup sugar
3 tablespoons ground cinnamon

1 Preheat the oven to 350°. Beat first 5 ingredients at high speed of an electric beater 3 minutes. Pour half of batter evenly into 2 greased and floured 4" x 8" disposable loafpans.

2 Stir together sugar and cinnamon in a small bowl; sprinkle half of sugar mixture evenly over batter in loafpans. Pour remaining batter evenly into loafpans, and sprinkle evenly with remaining sugar mixture. Gently swirl with a knife.

3 Bake at 350° for 45 minutes or until a wooden toothpick inserted in center comes out clean. Cool in pans on wire racks. Store in freezer, if desired.

Take Five!

Follow these directions to make five little gift loaves: Pour half of batter evenly into five greased and floured 3¼" x 5¾" disposable loafpans. Sprinkle evenly with half of sugar mixture. Pour remaining batter into pans; sprinkle with remaining sugar mixture. Gently swirl with a knife. Bake at 350° for 35 minutes or until a wooden toothpick inserted in center comes out clean.

Orange-Almond Coffee Cake

8 servings

2   cups biscuit mix
⅔   cup orange juice
¼   cup sugar
2   tablespoons butter, melted
1   large egg, lightly beaten
¼   cup sliced almonds

1   tablespoon sugar
2   tablespoons orange juice

1 Preheat the oven to 400°. Combine first 5 ingredients. Spread batter in a lightly greased 9" round cakepan; sprinkle evenly with almonds.

2 Bake at 400° for 15 minutes or until a wooden toothpick inserted in center comes out clean.

3 Sprinkle cake with 1 tablespoon sugar, and drizzle with 2 tablespoons orange juice; bake 5 more minutes. Cut into wedges, and serve warm.

" This coffee cake is a great one to serve when you have the gals over. But don't wait for company to enjoy the orange and almond flavor of this simple treat. "

Sweet Inspiration

“You don't have to wait 'til after dinner to enjoy these mouth-watering treats— they're good any time of day!”

Tropical Breeze

8 servings

¾ cup orange liqueur
½ cup white crème de cacao
¼ cup amaretto
½ gallon vanilla ice cream, softened

1 Combine liqueurs; stir well. Process half the liqueur mixture and half the ice cream in container of an electric blender until smooth. Pour mixture into a 2-quart pitcher. Repeat procedure with remaining ingredients. Serve immediately in stemmed glasses.

"This drink is for adults only. So kick back and let a creamy Tropical Breeze take you on a dream vacation to the tropics—sans kids!"

Blueberry Cloud Parfaits

8 servings

¾ cup sugar
2 tablespoons cornstarch
2 cups milk
4 egg yolks, lightly beaten

3 tablespoons orange liqueur or
    orange juice
2 tablespoons butter
1½ teaspoons vanilla extract
1 cup whipping cream, whipped

4 cups fresh blueberries

1 Combine first 4 ingredients in a saucepan, stirring with a wire whisk until well blended. Cook over medium heat, stirring constantly, until mixture thickens and boils. Boil 1 minute, stirring constantly.

2 Remove from heat; add liqueur, butter, and vanilla, stirring until butter melts. Let cool completely; fold in whipped cream. Cover and chill thoroughly.

3 To serve, place ½ cup blueberries into each of 8 stemmed dessert glasses, and top with ½ cup whipped cream mixture.

Make a "Berry" Good Choice!
Fresh blueberries out of season? No problem! Just use whatever's on hand! Whole raspberries or blackberries taste equally wonderful, or you can slice up some plump strawberries to make this a year-round dessert!

Double Chocolate Pudding

8 servings

1 (3.4-ounce) package chocolate
   pudding mix
2 cups milk
1 cup (6 ounces) semisweet chocolate
   chips

1 Combine pudding mix and milk in a saucepan; stir well. Cook, stirring constantly, over medium heat until mixture comes to a boil; remove from heat. Add chocolate chips, stirring until chocolate melts.

2 Spoon mixture evenly into 8 (4-ounce) pots de crème cups or soufflé cups. Serve warm or chilled.

“Here's the ultimate indulgence for chocolate lovers! Serve it up in fancy schmancy dessert glasses. It's so-o-o easy!”

Apple Pie Pizzas

8 pizzas

2   tablespoons all-purpose flour
½   cup packed brown sugar
1   teaspoon ground cinnamon

1   (17.3-ounce) can refrigerated
     biscuits

1   cup (4 ounces) shredded Cheddar
     cheese
2   small cooking apples, peeled,
     cored, and sliced
¼   cup butter

1 Preheat the oven to 350°. Combine first 3 ingredients in a small bowl; stir well.

2 Roll biscuits into 4" circles, and place on a lightly greased baking sheet.

3 Sprinkle shredded cheese evenly over circles, leaving ¼" borders. Arrange apple slices over cheese. Sprinkle cinnamon mixture over apples, and dot with butter. Bake at 350° for 18 to 20 minutes.

> *" Everyone loves apple pie—even kids when you serve up this pizza-inspired variation! It's even great for breakfast! Just shape the novel pizzas from refrigerated biscuits and pile 'em with shredded cheese, apples, and a sprinkling of cinnamon sugar. "*

Mighty Marshmallow Crescent Puffs

16 servings

2 (8-ounce) cans refrigerated crescent rolls
¼ cup granulated sugar
1 teaspoon ground cinnamon

16 large marshmallows
¼ cup butter, melted

½ cup sifted powdered sugar
2 teaspoons milk
¼ cup chopped pecans

1 Preheat the oven to 375°. Unroll crescent roll dough, and separate into 16 triangles. Combine granulated sugar and cinnamon in a bowl.

2 For each puff, dip a marshmallow into melted butter, and dredge in cinnamon-sugar mixture. Place marshmallow on shortest side of a dough triangle; fold point of shortest side over marshmallow, and roll toward opposite point, covering marshmallow. Pinch seams to seal. Dip 1 side of puff in melted butter, and place buttered side down in an ungreased muffin cup.

3 Bake at 375° for 12 to 15 minutes or until puffed and golden. Remove from pans immediately. Combine powdered sugar and milk; drizzle over warm puffs. Sprinkle with pecans.

❝ These puffy pastries are as much fun to make as they are to eat, so get the kids in on the action! Let 'em dip the marshmallows in butter and dredge 'em in cinnamon sugar. ❞

Ice Cream Dream

8 servings

½ gallon vanilla ice cream, softened
1 cup large pecan pieces, toasted
1 cup flaked coconut, toasted
¼ cup brandy or 2 teaspoons brandy flavoring

1 Combine all ingredients in a large freezer-proof bowl; cover and freeze at least 5 hours.

Double 'em Up!

Toasting brings out the flavor of the nuts and coconut in this soft-serve ice cream, but it doesn't have to be time-consuming. In fact, you can do it in double time! Just toast your pecans and coconut on opposite ends of a rimmed baking sheet at the same time at 350° for 7 minutes, stirring the coconut after 5 minutes.

Almond-Ginger Ice Cream Sandwiches

8 servings

2 cups vanilla ice cream, softened
1/3 cup finely chopped almonds, toasted
1/8 teaspoon almond extract
16 (2"-round) thin gingersnaps

1 Combine first 3 ingredients in a bowl, stirring well. Spread 1/4 cup ice cream mixture onto each of 8 gingersnaps; top with remaining gingersnaps. Place on a baking sheet, and freeze until firm. Serve immediately, or wrap sandwiches individually in plastic wrap; store in freezer.

My family loves these frozen goodies so much I can hardly keep my freezer stocked with 'em! I bet you'll never go back to those store-bought ice cream sandwiches again!

Banana Split Waffles

4 servings

4   frozen waffles, toasted
2   cups vanilla ice cream
2   ripe bananas, sliced
1   (8-ounce) can pineapple tidbits or
     crushed pineapple, drained
Chocolate syrup or hot fudge topping

1 Place 1 toasted waffle on each of 4 dessert plates. Place a ½ cup of ice cream on each waffle. Top each serving with banana slices, pineapple, and chocolate syrup. Serve immediately.

Split Decision

Waffles furnish a crispy base for this breakfast bread-turned-dessert. Feel free to substitute chopped maraschino cherries or sliced strawberries for the pineapple if you'd like. Or offer all three and let others decide!

Crackly Sauce for Ice Cream

4 to 6 servings

1 cup packed brown sugar
¼ cup butter
2 tablespoons molasses
1½ tablespoons water
⅛ teaspoon salt
1 tablespoon white vinegar
⅓ cup sliced almonds, toasted

1 Combine first 6 ingredients in a small saucepan; cook over medium heat, stirring constantly, 9 minutes or until mixture reaches soft crack stage or candy thermometer registers 280°. Remove from heat; stir in almonds. Spoon immediately over ice cream.

Make this when you and a couple of friends are in the mood for something crunchy and chock-full of toasted nuts. The warm sauce crackles when it hits cold ice cream. The contrast is so incredible you'll want to eat it all, which is a good thing, since leftovers don't reheat well.

Triple Chocolate Cake

1 (10") cake

1 (18.25-ounce) package chocolate
   cake mix
1 (3.9-ounce) package chocolate
   instant pudding mix
2 cups (12 ounces) semisweet
   chocolate chips
1 (8-ounce) container sour cream
4 large eggs
½ cup chopped pecans
½ cup water
½ cup vegetable oil

Powdered sugar

1 Preheat the oven to 350°. Combine first 8 ingredients in a large bowl; stir with a wire whisk until ingredients are blended. Pour batter into a well-greased 12-cup Bundt pan.

2 Bake at 350° for 1 hour or until cake begins to pull away from sides of pan. Cool in pan on a wire rack 15 minutes; remove cake from pan, and cool completely on wire rack. Sift a small amount of powdered sugar over cake.

❝Chocolate cake mix and chocolate instant pudding mix add to the convenience of this rich, moist Bundt cake. The final chocolate in the trio? A full 2 cups of chips melt throughout the cake as it bakes!❞

Nutty Graham Picnic Cake

(pictured on page 174)
1 (10") cake

1   cup butter, softened
1½   cups packed brown sugar
3   large eggs

2   cups self-rising flour
1   cup cinnamon-flavored graham
        cracker crumbs
1   cup orange juice
1½   cups chopped pecans, toasted and
        divided

1   cup sifted powdered sugar
4   to 6 teaspoons milk

---

1 Preheat the oven to 350°. Beat butter in a large bowl at medium speed of an electric beater until creamy; gradually add brown sugar, beating well. Add eggs, 1 at a time, beating after each addition.

2 Combine flour and cracker crumbs; add to butter mixture alternately with orange juice, beginning and ending with flour mixture. Mix at low speed after each addition until blended. Stir in 1 cup pecans. Pour batter into a greased and floured 10" tube pan.

3 Bake at 350° for 48 to 50 minutes or until a wooden toothpick inserted in center comes out clean. (Cake will not rise to top of pan.) Cool in pan on a wire rack 15 minutes; remove from pan, and let cool completely on wire rack.

4 Stir together powdered sugar and enough milk to make a good drizzling consistency. Drizzle over cooled cake, and sprinkle with remaining ½ cup pecans.

Cinnamon Cinch

Cinnamon-flavored graham crackers enrich this cake with homespun flavor. But don't worry if you don't have the cinnamon variety; just stir ½ teaspoon ground cinnamon in with the flour.

Pineapple Cream Cake

15 servings

1 (15-ounce) can crushed pineapple, undrained

1 (18.25-ounce) package yellow cake mix
2 large eggs
1 (11-ounce) can mandarin oranges, drained
½ cup mayonnaise

1 (12-ounce) container frozen whipped topping, thawed
1 (5.1-ounce) package vanilla instant pudding mix

1 Preheat the oven to 350°. Drain pineapple, reserving juice; set pineapple aside.

2 Combine pineapple juice, cake mix, eggs, mandarin oranges, and mayonnaise in a large mixing bowl. Beat at medium speed of an electric beater until blended. Pour batter into a greased 9" x 13" baking dish. Bake at 350° for 30 minutes or until a wooden toothpick inserted in center comes out clean. Cool in dish on a wire rack.

3 Combine drained pineapple, whipped topping, and pudding mix in a mixing bowl; beat at low speed until blended. Spread mixture evenly over cake. Cover and chill at least 1 hour before serving. Store in refrigerator.

"Need a yummy dessert for a covered-dish supper? Then this is your ticket! You can even make it a day or two ahead, and grab it from the fridge on your way out the door!"

Streusel Shortcake

(pictured on page 4)
1 (8") cake

3   cups biscuit mix
⅔   cup milk
¼   cup butter, melted

½   cup packed brown sugar
½   cup chopped walnuts
¼   cup butter

1   (8-ounce) container frozen whipped
      topping, thawed
2   pints fresh strawberries, sliced

1 Preheat the oven to 400°. Combine first 3 ingredients in a large bowl; stir until a soft dough forms. Spread dough evenly in 2 greased 8" square pans.

2 Combine brown sugar and walnuts; cut in ¼ cup butter with pastry blender until mixture is crumbly. Sprinkle nut mixture over dough. Bake, uncovered, at 400° for 18 minutes or until a wooden toothpick inserted in center comes out clean. Cool in pans on wire racks 10 minutes; remove from pans, and cool completely on wire racks.

3 Place 1 cake layer on a serving plate. Spread half the whipped topping over cake layer, and arrange half the sliced strawberries on top. Repeat procedure with remaining layer, whipped topping, and strawberries. Chill until ready to serve.

A Matter of Berries

Prefer another type of berry? Bring on the blueberries. Or blackberries. Or any berry you like! This versatile shortcake tastes great with any type. Bet you'll like it with peaches, too!

Cookie Dough Cheesecake Squares

15 servings

2 (18-ounce) packages refrigerated sliceable chocolate chip cookie dough

2 (8-ounce) packages cream cheese, softened
½ cup sugar
2 large eggs
1 teaspoon vanilla extract

Slice 'n' bake cookies perform wonderful stunts as the crust and topping for these dessert cheesecake squares. You gotta taste 'em to believe it!

1 Preheat the oven to 350°. Cut 1 roll of cookie dough into 24 slices; arrange slices in a lightly greased 9" x 13" pan. Press slices together with fingers, covering bottom of pan to edges. Set pan aside.

2 Beat cream cheese at medium speed of an electric beater until creamy; gradually add sugar, beating well. Add eggs, 1 at a time, beating well after each addition. Add vanilla; beat well. Pour mixture over cookie dough in pan.

3 Cut remaining roll of cookie dough into 24 slices; arrange slices over cream cheese mixture. Bake at 350° for 45 minutes. Cool in pan on a wire rack. Cut into squares.

10-Minute Torte

10 servings

1   (10.75-ounce) loaf pound cake

1   teaspoon instant coffee granules
1   teaspoon hot water
1   (8-ounce) container sour cream
1   cup (6 ounces) semisweet chocolate
      chips, melted

1 Slice pound cake horizontally into 5 layers; set aside.

2 Combine coffee granules and hot water, stirring until granules dissolve. Stir coffee mixture and sour cream into melted chocolate. Spread chocolate mixture between layers and on top and sides of cake. Cover and chill thoroughly.

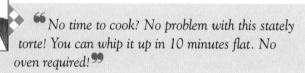

No time to cook? No problem with this stately torte! You can whip it up in 10 minutes flat. No oven required!

Flourless Chocolate Torte

(pictured on cover)
12 servings

2   (8-ounce) packages semisweet
    baking chocolate squares,
    chopped
1   cup butter
2   tablespoons coffee liqueur or 2
    tablespoons strong coffee, chilled

8   large eggs, separated
1½ cups sugar

Favorite chocolate sauce
Garnishes: frozen whipped topping,
           thawed; fresh raspberries;
           blueberries; and strawberries

1 Combine chocolate and butter in a large heavy saucepan. Cook and stir over low heat until melted. Remove from heat, and stir in liqueur; cool slightly.

2 Preheat the oven to 350°. Beat egg whites in a large mixing bowl at high speed of an electric beater just until stiff peaks form. Beat egg yolks and sugar in a large mixing bowl at medium speed until thick and pale. Fold one-third of chocolate mixture into yolk mixture. Gently fold in one-third of egg whites. Fold in remaining chocolate mixture and egg whites. Pour batter into a greased and floured 10-inch springform pan.

3 Bake at 350° for 30 minutes or until edges are set (center will not be set). Remove from oven, and gently run a knife around edge of pan to release torte. Cool to room temperature in pan on a wire rack; cover and chill 8 hours. Remove sides of pan just before serving. Serve with warm chocolate sauce; garnish, if desired.

" This decadent chocolate dessert is similar to a souf-flé, so expect it to fall slightly and to crack on top shortly after removing it from the oven. "

Caramel Apple Cobbler

15 servings

8	medium cooking apples, peeled, cored, and thinly sliced
½	cup granulated sugar
1	teaspoon ground cinnamon

1	cup packed brown sugar
¾	cup all-purpose flour
½	cup butter, softened
¾	cup quick-cooking oats, uncooked

Vanilla ice cream

1 Preheat the oven to 400°. Place apple slices in a lightly greased 9" x 13" pan. Combine granulated sugar and cinnamon; sprinkle over apples, tossing gently to coat.

2 Combine brown sugar and flour; cut in butter with pastry blender until mixture is crumbly. Stir in oats. Sprinkle brown sugar mixture evenly over apple mixture. Bake at 400° for 30 minutes. Serve warm with ice cream.

Apple Pickin' Time
Cooking apples work best in pies and cobblers like this. Pick from the following varieties at the market produce counter: Granny Smith, McIntosh, Rome Beauty, Stayman, Winesap, or York Imperial.

Blueberry Icebox Pie

2 (9") pies

2 (14-ounce) cans sweetened
      condensed milk
⅔ cup lemon juice
1 teaspoon vanilla extract
1 teaspoon almond extract
1 (12-ounce) container frozen
      whipped topping, thawed
1 (15½-ounce) can blueberries in
      syrup, drained (not pie filling)

2 (6-ounce) graham cracker crusts

1 Combine first 4 ingredients in a large bowl; stir well. Fold in whipped topping. Gently fold in blueberries.

2 Spoon mixture evenly into crusts. Cover and chill at least 3 hours.

❝ I use canned blueberries to make a nice variation from the traditional lemon icebox pie. The recipe makes two pies—one to keep and one to give away! ❞

Frosty Black Russian Pie

(pictured on facing page)
1 (9") pie

21   cream-filled chocolate sandwich
      cookies, finely crushed
3   tablespoons butter, melted

24   large marshmallows
½   cup milk

⅓   cup coffee liqueur or ⅓ cup strong
      coffee, chilled
1   cup whipping cream, whipped
Garnish: chocolate curls

1 Combine cookie crumbs and butter; stir well. Firmly press mixture in bottom and up sides of a 9" pie plate. Freeze 30 minutes or until firm.

2 Combine marshmallows and milk in a large heavy saucepan; cook over low heat until marshmallows melt, stirring constantly. Let cool in pan 1 hour.

3 Stir in liqueur. Gently fold whipped cream into marshmallow mixture. Chill 30 minutes; spoon into prepared crust. Cover and freeze 8 hours or until firm. Garnish, if desired.

Curls in a Whirl

Whip up fancy little chocolate curls by pulling a vegetable peeler down the flat side of a milk chocolate candy bar, and voila! It takes a little practice, so eat your mistakes and keep on pullin'! If you're in a hurry, just grate some chocolate over this pie—it'll taste just as yummy!

Nutty Graham Picnic Cake, page 164

Poinsettia Cookies, page 187

Quick 'n' Easy Pie

(pictured on facing page)
1 (9") pie

1 quart vanilla ice cream, softened
1 (6-ounce) chocolate crumb crust
1 (14.5-ounce) jar milk chocolate ice cream topping
3 (1.4-ounce) English toffee candy bars, chopped
Maraschino cherries with stems (optional)

1 Spread vanilla ice cream in crumb crust. Cover and freeze until ice cream is firm. Spread 1 cup ice cream topping over ice cream; sprinkle with chopped candy, and drizzle with remaining ice cream topping. Top each serving with a maraschino cherry, if desired. Serve immediately.

" My four-ingredient pie is a lip-smackin', make-ahead wonder. See for yourself! "

Toffee Ice Cream Pie

1 (9") pie

1 ⅓ cups vanilla wafer crumbs
¼ cup butter, melted

1 quart vanilla ice cream, softened
1 (10-ounce) package almond brickle
chips

⅔ cup sugar
½ cup evaporated milk
2 tablespoons butter
2 tablespoons light corn syrup

1 Preheat the oven to 375°. Combine wafer crumbs and melted butter; press firmly in bottom and up sides of a 9" pie plate. Bake at 375° for 8 minutes. Cool completely.

2 Combine softened ice cream and half the package of brickle chips; spoon into prepared crust. Cover and freeze until ice cream is firm.

3 Combine sugar and next 3 ingredients in a small saucepan; bring to a boil over low heat, stirring constantly. Cook 1 minute. Remove from heat, and stir in remaining half of brickle chips. Let sauce cool, stirring occasionally. Serve with pie.

" A buttery sauce drizzled over frozen ice cream pie with brickle chips doubles the toffee flavor of this divine dessert. Find the brickle chips on the baking aisle with the chocolate chips. "

178

Peppermint Pie

1 (9") pie

2 cups (12 ounces) semisweet
   chocolate chips, divided
6 tablespoons butter, divided
2 cups crisp rice cereal
½ cup chopped walnuts, toasted

1 quart peppermint ice cream,
   softened

½ cup milk
Crushed hard peppermint candy

1 Cook 1 cup chocolate chips and 2 tablespoons butter in a large saucepan over medium heat until chocolate and butter melt, stirring occasionally. Remove from heat. Stir in cereal and walnuts. Firmly press cereal mixture in bottom and up sides of a greased 9" pie plate. Chill until firm.

2 Spoon softened ice cream into prepared crust. Cover and freeze until ice cream is firm.

3 Just before serving, combine remaining 1 cup chocolate chips, remaining 4 tablespoons butter, and the milk in a small saucepan. Cook over low heat, stirring constantly, until chocolate and butter melt. Set aside, and let cool. Let pie stand at room temperature 5 minutes before serving. Drizzle chocolate mixture over pie; sprinkle with crushed candy.

" Crushed hard peppermint candy sprinkled over the top of this pie leaves no question as to the flavor inside! If you can't find peppermint ice cream, just substitute mint chocolate chip ice cream. "

Apricot-Pecan-Brie Tartlets

2 dozen

1   (8-ounce) round Brie, chilled

1½ (17¼-ounce) packages frozen puff
       pastry sheets, thawed

⅓   cup apricot preserves
24 pecan halves, toasted

*66 These little tarts make a
great not-so-sweet dessert for
a wine and cheese party. You can
even vary the flavor of the preserves,
if you'd like!99*

1 Preheat the oven to 425°. Slice rind
from cheese; cut cheese into 24
cubes, and set aside.

2 Roll each pastry sheet into a 10" x 15"
rectangle on a lightly floured surface;
cut each sheet into 8 squares. Fit squares
into miniature (1¾") muffin pans,
extending corners slightly above cup
rims. Bake pastry at 425° for 10 to 12
minutes or until it begins to brown.
Remove from oven, and gently press
handle of a wooden spoon into center of
each pastry, forming tart shells.

3 Spoon ½ teaspoon preserves into
each shell; top with a cheese cube
and a pecan half. Bake 5 more minutes
or until cheese melts; serve immediately.

Almond-Cherry Cobbler

6 servings

¼ cup butter

¾ cup all-purpose flour
1 teaspoon baking powder
¼ teaspoon salt
½ cup sugar
½ cup milk
¼ teaspoon almond extract
1 (16-ounce) can pitted tart red
   cherries, undrained (not pie filling)

1 Preheat the oven to 350°. Place butter in an 8" square baking dish. Place dish in oven at 350° for 5 minutes or until butter melts.

2 Combine flour and next 3 ingredients in a medium bowl; add milk and almond extract, stirring until smooth. Pour batter over melted butter. (Do not stir.) Pour cherries over batter.

3 Bake at 350° for 40 minutes or until lightly browned. Serve warm.

This cobbler goes together in a snap—let it cook while you enjoy dinner, and it'll be ready just in time for dessert. Crown each serving with a scoop of ice cream. M-m-m!

Gingered Peach Crisp

4 servings

2 (16-ounce) cans sliced peaches in heavy syrup, undrained

½ cup crushed gingersnap cookies (about 8 cookies)
2 tablespoons brown sugar
1 tablespoon butter, melted

1 Preheat the oven to 375°. Drain peaches, reserving ½ cup syrup. Place peaches and reserved syrup in a lightly greased 8" square baking dish.

2 Combine cookie crumbs, brown sugar, and butter; sprinkle over peaches. Bake at 375° for 20 minutes or until bubbly. Serve with ice cream.

"Crumbled gingersnaps make a peach of a crisp in this four-ingredient family favorite. Who says you don't have time to prepare dessert?"

Cookie Jar Jubilee

“It's hard to resist this scrumptious collection of cookies and candies—so don't! Whip up a batch for your gang today!”

Lemon Crispies

about 3 dozen

¾ cup shortening
1 cup sugar
3 large eggs

2 cups all-purpose flour
¾ teaspoon baking soda
⅛ teaspoon salt
2 (3.4-ounce) packages lemon instant
    pudding mix

1 Preheat the oven to 375°. Beat shortening in a large bowl at medium speed of an electric beater until fluffy. Gradually add sugar, beating well. Add eggs, 1 at a time, beating well after each addition.

2 Combine flour and remaining 3 ingredients in a medium bowl; gradually add to shortening mixture, beating well. Drop dough by rounded teaspoonfuls onto lightly greased cookie sheets. Bake at 375° for 8 to 9 minutes or until lightly browned. Cool 1 minute on cookie sheets; transfer cookies to wire racks to cool completely.

" No need to squeeze fresh lemons for these cookies. Lemon pudding mix packs the tart punch in this recipe! "

Chocolate Macaroons

about 3 dozen

1   cup (6 ounces) semisweet chocolate
     chips
1   cup flaked coconut
½   cup finely chopped walnuts

2   egg whites
¼   teaspoon salt
½   cup sugar

1 Melt chocolate in a large heavy saucepan over low heat. Let cool to room temperature. Stir in coconut and walnuts.

2 Preheat the oven to 350°. Beat egg whites and salt in a small bowl at high speed of an electric beater until foamy. Gradually add sugar, 1 tablespoon at a time, beating until stiff peaks form and sugar dissolves (2 to 4 minutes). Fold egg white mixture into chocolate mixture. Drop by rounded teaspoonfuls onto cookie sheets lined with aluminum foil. Bake at 350° for 10 minutes. Cool 1 minute on cookie sheets; transfer cookies to wire racks to cool completely.

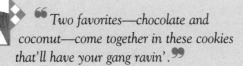

Two favorites—chocolate and coconut—come together in these cookies that'll have your gang ravin'.

Easy Peanut Butter Cookies

about 5½ dozen

1   (14-ounce) can sweetened
      condensed milk
¾ cup creamy peanut butter
2   cups biscuit mix
1   teaspoon vanilla extract

Sugar
About 66 milk chocolate kisses,
    unwrapped (optional)

1 Combine condensed milk and peanut butter in a large bowl. Beat at medium speed of an electric beater until well blended. Add biscuit mix and vanilla; beat well.

2 Preheat the oven to 375°. Shape mixture into 1" balls; roll in sugar. Place 2" apart on ungreased cookie sheets. Dip a fork in sugar; flatten cookies in a crisscross design.

3 Bake at 375° for 6 to 7 minutes. Immediately press a chocolate kiss in center of each cookie after removing from oven, if desired. Transfer cookies to wire racks to cool completely.

Wanna Kiss?
These cookies are good with or without chocolate kisses—either way, you have a winner!

Poinsettia Cookies

(pictured on page 175)
about 5 dozen

2   cups butter, softened
2   cups sifted powdered sugar
2   large eggs
1   teaspoon vanilla extract

3   cups all-purpose flour
1   teaspoon salt
1   cup flaked coconut
1   cup (6 ounces) butterscotch chips, divided

Sugar
1   (4-ounce) container red candied cherries, cut into wedges

1 Beat butter at medium speed of an electric beater until creamy; gradually add powdered sugar, beating well. Add eggs and vanilla, beating well.

2 Combine flour and salt in a medium bowl; add to butter mixture, beating well. Stir in flaked coconut and ¾ cup butterscotch chips. Cover and chill at least 8 hours.

3 Preheat the oven to 350°. Shape dough into 1" balls; place on ungreased cookie sheets. Dip a flat-bottomed glass in sugar, and flatten each ball into a 2" circle. Place a butterscotch chip in the center of each cookie. Arrange 5 cherry wedges in a circular pattern around each butterscotch chip to resemble a poinsettia. Bake at 350° for 9 to 10 minutes. Cool 1 minute on cookie sheets; transfer cookies to wire racks to cool completely.

" These pretty cookies are named for the decorative flower design made from red candied cherry wedges and butterscotch chips on top of each one. Aren't they cute?!"

Pecan Biscotti

about 2½ dozen

1¾ cups all-purpose flour
½ cup yellow cornmeal
1¼ teaspoons baking powder
¼ teaspoon salt
1 cup finely chopped pecans
¾ cup sugar
½ cup vegetable oil
2 large eggs

1 Preheat the oven to 350°. Combine first 5 ingredients in a large bowl. Combine sugar, oil, and eggs in a medium bowl; gradually add to flour mixture, stirring just until dry ingredients are moistened.

2 Place dough on a lightly floured surface; divide in half. With lightly floured hands, shape each portion of dough into a 1¼" x 12" log. Place logs 3" apart on a lightly greased cookie sheet. Bake at 350° for 25 minutes. Cool completely on cookie sheet.

3 Cut each log crosswise into ¾"-thick slices, using a serrated knife. Place slices, cut sides down, on cookie sheets. Bake at 350° for 15 minutes, turning cookies once. Cool slightly on cookie sheets; transfer cookies to wire racks to cool completely.

66 The texture of these crisp little cookies makes 'em perfect for dunkin' in a cup of coffee for a sweet little breakfast or an afternoon pick-me-up! 99

Brickle Bars

about 2 dozen

1   (18.25-ounce) package yellow cake
    mix without pudding
⅓   cup butter, melted
1   large egg, lightly beaten

1   (10-ounce) package almond brickle
    chips
1   (14-ounce) can sweetened
    condensed milk
½   cup chopped pecans

1 Preheat the oven to 350°. Combine first 3 ingredients in a large bowl, stirring mixture well. Gently press into a 9" x 13" pan.

2 Combine brickle chips, condensed milk, and pecans in a medium bowl; spread over crust in pan. Bake at 350° for 25 minutes. Cool in pan on a wire rack; cut into bars.

" A box of cake mix is the quick secret to these chewy Brickle Bars. Shhh! Don't tell anyone how easy they are! Tip: Find the brickle chips on the baking aisle by their chocolate cousins!"

Speedy Little Devils

about 3 dozen

1   (18.25-ounce) package devil's food
    cake mix
½   cup butter, melted

½   cup creamy peanut butter
1   (7-ounce) jar marshmallow creme

1 Preheat the oven to 350°. Combine cake mix and butter in a large bowl, stirring well (mixture will be crumbly). Set aside 1½ cups cake mixture. Press remaining cake mixture into a greased 9" x 13" pan.

2 Combine peanut butter and marshmallow creme in a small bowl, stirring until blended. Dollop peanut butter mixture evenly over mixture in pan; spread evenly, using back of a spoon. Sprinkle reserved 1½ cups cake mixture over peanut butter mixture. Bake, uncovered, at 350° for 20 minutes. Cool in pan on a wire rack. Cut into bars.

"Devil's food cake mix bakes into delightful brownies with an extra temptation—a ribbon of peanut butter and marshmallow creme in the center. Now who can resist these?"

Sinful Seven-Layer Cookies

about 1 ¼ dozen

½ cup butter

1 cup graham cracker crumbs

1 cup (6 ounces) semisweet chocolate chips

1 cup (6 ounces) butterscotch chips

1 cup flaked coconut, toasted

1 (14-ounce) can sweetened condensed milk

1 cup chopped pecans

1 Preheat the oven to 350°. Place butter in a 9" x 13" baking dish. Place dish in oven at 350° for 5 minutes or until butter melts. Layer graham cracker crumbs and next 3 ingredients over butter. Pour condensed milk over coconut; top with pecans. Bake at 350° for 30 minutes. Cool in dish on a wire rack; cut into squares.

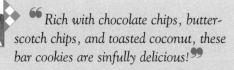

Rich with chocolate chips, butterscotch chips, and toasted coconut, these bar cookies are sinfully delicious!

Peanut Butter S'More Bars

about 2 dozen

½   cup butter, softened
1   cup packed brown sugar
½   cup chunky peanut butter
1   large egg
½   teaspoon vanilla extract
1½ cups self-rising flour

1   (7-ounce) jar marshmallow creme
1   cup (6 ounces) semisweet chocolate
      chips
¾   cup salted roasted peanuts

1 Preheat the oven to 375°. Beat butter at medium speed of an electric beater until creamy; add brown sugar, beating well. Add peanut butter, egg, and vanilla; beat well. Add flour to butter mixture, beating well.

2 Press dough into a greased 9" x 13" pan. Spread marshmallow creme over dough. Sprinkle chocolate chips and peanuts over marshmallow creme. Bake at 375° for 15 minutes or until marshmallow creme is lightly browned. Cool in pan on a wire rack; cut into bars.

❝You can enjoy this cookie version of the favorite campfire treat in the comfort of your own home! My rendition has a chunky peanut butter crust that's layered with marshmallow creme, chocolate, and peanuts. OOH IT'S SO GOOD!!❞

Stir 'n' Bake Bars

about 2 dozen

1	cup flaked coconut
½	cup quick-cooking oats, uncooked
½	cup packed brown sugar
⅓	cup water
2	large eggs, lightly beaten
1	(18.25-ounce) package chocolate or yellow butter recipe cake mix with pudding

¼	cup chopped pecans
1	tablespoon granulated sugar

1 Preheat the oven to 350°. Combine first 6 ingredients in a large bowl; pour into a lightly greased 9" x 13" pan.

2 Combine pecans and granulated sugar in a small bowl; sprinkle evenly over batter. Bake at 350° for 20 to 25 minutes or until golden. Cool in pan on a wire rack. Cut into bars.

Flavor Teaser

You pick the flavor of these cake mix-inspired bar cookies. They're equally yummy with a chocolate or butter recipe cake mix!

No-Bake Brownies

about 3 dozen

2 cups (12 ounces) semisweet
   chocolate chips
1 cup evaporated milk

1 (11-ounce) package vanilla wafers

2 cups miniature marshmallows
1 cup chopped pecans
1 cup sifted powdered sugar

2 teaspoons evaporated milk

1 Combine chocolate chips and 1 cup evaporated milk in a large heavy saucepan; cook over low heat until chocolate melts, stirring occasionally. Set aside.

2 Process vanilla wafers, in 2 batches, in a food processor to make coarse crumbs. Place crumbs in a large bowl.

3 Stir marshmallows, pecans, and powdered sugar into crumbs. Reserve ½ cup chocolate mixture. Stir remaining chocolate mixture into crumb mixture. Press mixture into a well-greased 9" square pan.

4 Combine reserved ½ cup chocolate mixture and 2 teaspoons evaporated milk in a small bowl; spread over crumb mixture. Cover and chill at least 1 hour. Cut into squares.

" I love these no-bake brownies, and you will, too! They heat on the cooktop just long enough to melt the chocolate. But that's it—there's no need to heat up the kitchen with the oven! "

Peanutty Candy Bar Brownies

about 3 dozen

1 (19.8-ounce) package fudge brownie mix
¼ cup vegetable oil
½ cup creamy peanut butter
3 (7-ounce) peanuts in milk chocolate candy bars

1 Preheat the oven to 350°. Prepare brownie mix batter in a large bowl according to package directions, using ¼ cup oil. Stir peanut butter into batter. Spread half of brownie batter into an ungreased 9" x 13" baking pan. Place whole candy bars across batter. Spread remaining batter over candy bars.

2 Bake at 350° for 28 to 30 minutes. Cool in pan on a wire rack. (See box below.) Cut into squares.

" These brownies have a gooey center when served warm. The longer they cool, the firmer the candy bar center becomes. If you can't find the 7-ounce candy bars, just use 2 (10-ounce) packages, and stack 'em in two layers over half the brownie batter. Best of all, either way you make 'em or eat 'em, they're so-o-o good!"

Gooey Mocha Brownies

about 1 ½ dozen

1 ½ cups sugar
¾ cup butter
¼ cup strong coffee
2 cups (12 ounces) semisweet chocolate chips
4 large eggs, lightly beaten

1 ½ cups all-purpose flour
½ teaspoon baking soda
½ teaspoon salt
1 cup chopped pecans

1 Preheat the oven to 350°. Combine first 3 ingredients in a large saucepan. Bring to a boil, stirring often. Remove from heat. Add chocolate chips; stir until chocolate melts. Add eggs, stirring well.

2 Combine flour, baking soda, and salt in a medium bowl; add to chocolate mixture, stirring well. Add pecans. Spoon into a greased 9" x 13" pan. Bake at 350° for 30 minutes. Cool in pan on a wire rack. Cut into squares.

❝ If you're fond of a fudgy brownie, you'll love these. Just beware—they're so gooey you may have trouble cutting them into squares. The only other trouble you may have is havin' 'em disappear too fast! ❞

White Chocolate Fudge

1 ½ pounds

6   ounces premium white chocolate, chopped

½   (8-ounce) package cream cheese, softened
3   cups sifted powdered sugar
½   teaspoon vanilla extract
1   cup chopped pecans

25   pecan halves

1 Cook white chocolate in a small heavy saucepan over low heat until melted, stirring occasionally. Remove from heat.

2 Beat cream cheese in a large bowl at high speed of an electric beater until creamy. Gradually add powdered sugar; beat at medium speed until smooth. Stir in chocolate and vanilla; beat well. Stir in chopped pecans.

3 Press mixture into a lightly buttered 8" square pan. Cover and chill. Cut into 25 squares. Gently press a pecan half onto each square of fudge. Store in an airtight container in the refrigerator.

"I betcha gonna love this easy, no-cook fudge as much I do—all you have to do is melt the white chocolate and then beat it into the other ingredients! The white chocolate makes it extra yummy—you won't keep this batch of confections around for long!"

Peanut Butter Cups

about 4 dozen

⅔ cup creamy peanut butter
½ cup sifted powdered sugar
2 teaspoons vanilla extract

16 ounces chocolate-flavored bark candy coating squares or semi-sweet chocolate squares
48 (1½") paper candy cups

1 Combine first 3 ingredients in a small bowl; stir well. Cover and chill 1 hour or until firm. Shape mixture by teaspoonfuls into balls, and flatten slightly.

2 Melt candy coating in a small microwave-safe bowl according to package directions. Spoon ½ teaspoon melted candy coating into 48 paper-lined miniature (1¾") muffin cups. Place 1 peanut butter ball in each cup; spoon remaining melted candy coating over peanut butter balls to cover completely. Cover and chill until firm. Store in an airtight container in refrigerator.

Sweet Treats for Your Valentine!
Oh, how pretty these look in the decorative little candy cups. Pack several in little heart-shaped boxes for all the special people in your life!

Microwave Pralines

about 2½ dozen

2   cups sugar
2   cups pecans, chopped
1   (5-ounce) can evaporated milk
¼   cup butter
1   tablespoon vanilla extract

1 Combine all ingredients in a 2-quart microwave-safe glass measuring cup. Microwave at **HIGH** 5 to 6 minutes, stirring well. Microwave 5 to 6 more minutes, stirring well. Working rapidly, drop by tablespoonfuls onto wax paper; let stand until firm.

If you thought pralines were hard to make, try my microwave version! They turn out perfect every time. If your oven is 1,000 watts, use the lowest cooking time option.

Rocky Road Clusters

about 3 dozen

2   cups (12 ounces) semisweet
     chocolate chips

1   cup miniature marshmallows
½   cup slivered almonds, toasted

1 Cook chocolate chips in a large heavy saucepan over low heat until chocolate melts, stirring occasionally. Set aside, and cool.

2 Add marshmallows and almonds to chocolate; stir well. Drop by teaspoonfuls onto wax paper. Chill 15 minutes or until firm. Store in an airtight container in the refrigerator.

Chocolate Tip!
Let the melted chocolate cool just enough so it doesn't melt the marshmallows when you stir 'em together. Get the picture?

Chewy Chocolate Crunch

about 2½ pounds

2   cups (12 ounces) semisweet chocolate chips
1   (11-ounce) package butterscotch chips
1   (16-ounce) jar unsalted roasted peanuts
1   (5-ounce) can chow mein noodles

1 Lightly grease an aluminum foil-lined baking sheet. Combine chocolate and butterscotch chips in a large microwave-safe bowl. Microwave at HIGH 2½ to 3½ minutes or until chips melt; stir well. Add peanuts to melted mixture, stirring to coat. Add noodles; gently stir to coat.

2 Pour mixture onto baking sheet, spreading evenly over surface with back of a spoon. Cover and chill at least 8 hours. Break into pieces.

66 *Chocolate and butterscotch chips provide the 'chewy' and peanuts and chow mein noodles contribute the 'crunch' to this betcha-can't-eat-just-one candy.* 99

Coconut Joys

about 3½ dozen

½ cup butter
2 cups sifted powdered sugar
3 cups flaked coconut

⅓ cup (2 ounces) semisweet chocolate chips

1 Melt butter in a saucepan over low heat; remove from heat. Stir in powdered sugar and coconut; shape into ¾" balls. Chill until firm.

2 Place chocolate chips in a small heavy-duty, zip-top plastic bag; seal. Submerge in hot water until chocolate melts. Snip a tiny hole in 1 corner of bag, and drizzle chocolate over coconut balls. Let candies stand until firm; store in refrigerator.

Joy of Chocolate
If extra chocolate is what you desire, you'll want to make Chocolate-Covered Coconut Joys. Simply microwave 2 cups (12 ounces) semisweet chocolate chips in a 2-cup glass measuring cup at HIGH 1½ minutes or until melted, stirring twice. Then dip coconut candies into melted chocolate, allowing excess to drip, and place on wax paper. Let candies stand until firm; store in refrigerator.

Tempt-Me Truffles

about 4 dozen

1   (8-ounce) package cream cheese, softened
4   cups sifted powdered sugar
5   (1-ounce) squares unsweetened chocolate, melted
1   teaspoon vanilla extract

Finely chopped toasted almonds
Unsweetened cocoa
Powdered sugar

1 Beat cream cheese at medium speed of an electric beater until creamy; gradually add 4 cups powdered sugar, beating well after each addition. Stir in melted chocolate and vanilla. Cover and chill 2 hours or until mixture is firm.

2 Shape mixture into 1" balls; roll some in almonds, some in cocoa, and some in powdered sugar. Cover and chill at least 1 hour; serve chilled. Store in an airtight container in refrigerator.

"These elegant chocolate candies are deceptively easy to make. Finely chopped toasted almonds, unsweetened cocoa, and powdered sugar offer different looks and textures and cloak the truffles in style!"

METRIC EQUIVALENTS

The recipes that appear in this cookbook use the standard United States method for measuring liquid and dry or solid ingredients (teaspoons, tablespoons, and cups). The information in the following charts is provided to help cooks outside the U.S. successfully use these recipes. All equivalents are approximate.

EQUIVALENTS FOR DIFFERENT TYPES OF INGREDIENTS

A standard cup measure of a dry or solid ingredient will vary in weight depending on the type of ingredient. A standard cup of liquid is the same volume for any type of liquid. Use the following chart when converting standard cup measures to grams (weight) or milliliters (volume).

Standard Cup	Fine Powder (ex. flour)	Grain (ex. rice)	Granular (ex. sugar)	Liquid Solids (ex. butter)	Liquid (ex. milk)
1	140 g	150 g	190 g	200 g	240 ml
¾	105 g	113 g	143 g	150 g	180 ml
⅔	93 g	100 g	125 g	133 g	160 ml
½	70 g	75 g	95 g	100 g	120 ml
⅓	47 g	50 g	63 g	67 g	80 ml
¼	35 g	38 g	48 g	50 g	60 ml
⅛	18 g	19 g	24 g	25 g	30 ml

DRY INGREDIENTS BY WEIGHT

(To convert ounces to grams, multiply the number of ounces by 30.)

1 oz	=	¹⁄₁₆ lb	=	30 g
4 oz	=	¼ lb	=	120 g
8 oz	=	½ lb	=	240 g
12 oz	=	¾ lb	=	360 g
16 oz	=	1 lb	=	480 g

LENGTH

(To convert inches to centimeters, multiply the number of inches by 2.5.)

1 in			=	2.5 cm		
6 in	=	½ ft	=	15 cm		
12 in	=	1 ft	=	30 cm		
36 in	=	3 ft	= 1 yd =	90 cm		
40 in			=	100 cm	=	1 meter

LIQUID INGREDIENTS BY VOLUME

¼ tsp					=		1 ml	
½ tsp					=		2 ml	
1 tsp					=		5 ml	
3 tsp	=	1 tbls		=	½ fl oz	=	15 ml	
		2 tbls	=	⅛ cup	= 1 fl oz	=	30 ml	
		4 tbls	=	¼ cup	= 2 fl oz	=	60 ml	
		5⅓ tbls	=	⅓ cup	= 3 fl oz	=	80 ml	
		8 tbls	=	½ cup	= 4 fl oz	=	120 ml	
		10⅔ tbls	=	⅔ cup	= 5 fl oz	=	160 ml	
		12 tbls	=	¾ cup	= 6 fl oz	=	180 ml	
		16 tbls	=	1 cup	= 8 fl oz	=	240 ml	
		1 pt	=	2 cups	= 16 fl oz	=	480 ml	
		1 qt	=	4 cups	= 32 fl oz	=	960 ml	
					33 fl oz	=	1000 ml	= 1 liter

COOKING/OVEN TEMPERATURES

	Fahrenheit	Celsius	Gas Mark
Freeze Water	32° F	0° C	
Room Temperature	68° F	20° C	
Boil Water	212° F	100° C	
Bake	325° F	160° C	3
	350° F	180° C	4
	375° F	190° C	5
	400° F	200° C	6
	425° F	220° C	7
	450° F	230° C	8
Broil			Grill

Index

Almond Coffee Cake, Orange-, 152
Almond-Ginger Ice Cream Sandwiches, 160
Appetizers
  Cheese, Cranberry-Pecan Goat, 13
  Dips
    Guacamole, Jalapeño, 10
    Meaty Cheesy Dip, 11
    Pizzeria Dip, 12
  Fondue, Fast 'n' Fabulous, 14
  Muffins, Cheesy Cocktail, 19
  Peanuts, Hot Chili, 18
  Pineapple, Marinated, 15
  Roll-ups, Popeye's, 17
  Sandwiches, Cucumber, 16
  Soup, Cream of Pimiento, 116
  Squares, Pepperoni Pie, 21
  Tenders, Sesame Chicken, 22
  Wafers, Sesame Cheese, 20
  Wings, Balsamic Chicken, 23
Apple Cobbler, Caramel, 170
Apple Pie Pizzas, 157
Apricot Chicken, Sweet-and-Sour, 32
Apricot-Pecan-Brie Tartlets, 180
Artichoke Cream Sauce, Chicken with, 33
Asparagus and Goat Cheese Salad, 125
Asparagus with Blue Cheese Vinaigrette, 96

Bananas
  Muffins, Surprise 'Nana, 138
  Shake, PB 'n' Nanner, 27
  Waffles, Banana Split, 161
Beans
  "Baked" Beans, Quick, 97
  Green Beans, Lemon-Basil, 100
  Salad, Three-Bean and Cilantro, 126
Beef
  Sandwiches, Uptown Roast Beef, 77
  Sirloin Tips with Garlic Butter, 45
  Steaks
    Asian Beef and Noodles, Easy, 70
    au Vin, Beef Fillets, 44
    Porterhouse Steaks, Grilled, 43
    Tenderloin, Easy Beef, 42
Beef, Ground
  Burgers, Surprise, 74
  Chili, Super-Easy, 121
  Dip, Meaty Cheesy, 11
  Meatball Sandwiches, Mighty, 76
  Pie, Skillet Sombrero, 75

  Pizza, Bubble, 72
  Soup, Beef-Tortellini, 120
  Steak 'n' Gravy, Smothered, 71
  Stroganoff, 10-Minute, 73
Beverages
  Alcoholic
    Daiquiri, Frozen Mango, 30
    Nog, Holiday, 29
    Tropical Breeze, 154
  Cider, Hot Cran-Apple, 24
  Honeyade, Lemon, 26
  Piña Colada, Parson's, 28
  Shake, PB 'n' Nanner, 27
  Tea, Peachy, 25
Biscuits, Cheater's Beaten, 135
Biscuits, Cheese-Garlic, 134
Blueberry Cloud Parfaits, 155
Blueberry Icebox Pie, 171
Breads. *See also* Biscuits, Cornbread, Muffins.
  Beignets, 149
  Breadsticks, Butter-Me-Up, 140
  French Braid, Honey-Almond, 150
  French Bread, Double Cheese-Topped, 146
  French Bread, Fine Wine, 143
  Knots, Sesame, 141
  Loaf, Italian Pull-Apart, 145
  Loaves, Cinnamon, 151
  Popovers, Onion, 139
  "Salad" Bread, 147
  Scones, Dried Cherry, 136
  Sweet Rolls, Cranberry, 148
  Swirls, Quick 'n' Cheesy Bacon, 142
Broccoli Bake, Easy Cheesy, 98

Cakes
  Cheesecake Squares, Cookie Dough, 167
  Chocolate Cake, Triple, 163
  Coffee Cake, Orange-Almond, 152
  Picnic Cake, Nutty Graham, 164
  Pineapple Cream Cake, 165
  Shortcake, Streusel, 166
  Torte, Flourless Chocolate, 169
  Torte, 10-Minute, 168
Candies
  Clusters, Rocky Road, 200
  Crunch, Chewy Chocolate, 201
  Cups, Peanut Butter, 198
  Fudge, White Chocolate, 197
  Joys, Coconut, 202

Candies *(continued)*

Pralines, Microwave, 199
Truffles, Tempt-Me, 203
Cantaloupe Soup, Frosty, 114
Carrots, Devilish, 99
Casseroles
Broccoli Bake, Easy Cheesy, 98
Chicken Dinner, One-Pot, 67
Chicken Divan, Easy, 63
Chicken Manicotti with Chive Cream Sauce, 41
Chicken-Noodle Casserole, Chunky, 66
Eggplant Parmesan Express, 88
Mac 'n' Cheese, Sea Shell, 90
Pizza, Bubble, 72
Rice 'n' Cheese Casserole, Mexi, 94
Cheese. *See also* Appetizers.
Breads
Biscuits, Cheese-Garlic, 134
French Bread, Double Cheese-Topped, 146
Muffins, Cheesy Cocktail, 19
"Salad" Bread, 147
Swirls, Quick 'n' Cheesy Bacon, 142
Broccoli Bake, Easy Cheesy, 98
Burgers, Surprise, 74
Casserole, Mexi Rice 'n' Cheese, 94
Dip, Meaty Cheesy, 11
Eggplant Parmesan Express, 88
Flounder au Gratin, 52
Kabobs, Swiss-Ham, 82
Mac 'n' Cheese, Sea Shell, 90
Pasta with Tomatoes, Brie, and Basil, 59
Penne with Nutty Cream Sauce, Two-Cheese, 60
Pizza, Bubble, 72
Quesadillas, Mexi-Cheesy, 87
Salad, Asparagus and Goat Cheese, 125
Tartlets, Apricot-Pecan-Brie, 180
Turnovers, Sausage and Cheese, 80
Veal Parmigiana, 46
Cherry Cobbler, Almond-, 181
Cherry Scones, Dried, 136
Chicken. *See also* Turkey.
Artichoke Cream Sauce, Chicken with, 33
Asian Chicky, Slow-and-Easy, 36
Casserole, Chunky Chicken-Noodle, 66
Dinner, One-Pot Chicken, 67
Divan, Easy Chicken, 63
Florentine, Lasagna-Chicken, 58
Garlic-Lime Chicken-on-the-Grill, 64
Livers in Sour Cream, Chicken, 68
Manicotti with Chive Cream Sauce,
Chicken, 41

Marsala, Chicken, 35
Nuggets, Baked Chicken, 65
Piccata, Chicken, 62
Praline Chicken, 34
Soup, Mexican Chicken, 119
Sweet-and-Sour Apricot Chicken, 32
Tenders, Sesame Chicken, 22
Wings, Balsamic Chicken, 23
Chili, Super-Easy, 121
Chocolate
Bars and Cookies
Brownies, Gooey Mocha, 196
Brownies, No-Bake, 194
Brownies, Peanutty Candy Bar, 195
Devils, Speedy Little, 190
Layer Cookies, Sinful Seven-, 191
Macaroons, Chocolate, 185
Stir 'n' Bake Bars, 193
Cake, Triple Chocolate, 163
Candies
Clusters, Rocky Road, 200
Crunch, Chewy Chocolate, 201
Cups, Peanut Butter, 198
Fudge, White Chocolate, 197
Truffles, Tempt-Me, 203
Pie, Frosty Black Russian, 172
Pudding, Double Chocolate, 156
Torte, Flourless Chocolate, 169
Torte, 10-Minute, 168
Coconut Joys, 202
Cookies
Bars and Squares
Brickle Bars, 189
Brownies, Gooey Mocha, 196
Brownies, No-Bake, 194
Brownies, Peanutty Candy Bar, 195
Devils, Speedy Little, 190
Layer Cookies, Sinful Seven-, 191
S'More Bars, Peanut Butter, 192
Stir 'n' Bake Bars, 193
Biscotti, Pecan, 188
Crispies, Lemon, 184
Macaroons, Chocolate, 185
Peanut Butter Cookies, Easy, 186
Poinsettia Cookies, 187
Wafers, Sesame Cheese, 20
Corn and Crabmeat Soup, Easy, 118
Cornbread, Green Chilie, 144
Corn, Okra, and Tomatoes, 109
Crabmeat Soup, Easy Corn and, 118
Cranberries
Cheese, Cranberry-Pecan Goat, 13

Rolls, Cranberry Sweet, 148
Salad, Cranberry-Eggnog Gelatin, 122
Cucumber Sandwiches, 16

Desserts. *See also* Cakes, Cookies, Ice Cream,
Pies and Pastries.
Parfaits, Blueberry Cloud, 155
Pizzas, Apple Pie, 157
Pudding, Double Chocolate, 156
Sauce for Ice Cream, Crackly, 162
Waffles, Banana Split, 161

Egg Drop Soup, Chinese, 115
Eggplant Parmesan Express, 88

Fettuccine, Terrific Tuna, 84
Fish. *See also* Crab, Scallops, Shrimp.
Flounder au Gratin, 52
Grouper, Oriental, 53
Packets, Fish-in-Foil, 83
Salmon Steaks, Savory, 54
Tuna Fettuccine, Terrific, 84
Fondue, Fast 'n' Fabulous, 14

Guacamole, Jalapeño, 10

Ham. *See also* Pork.
Kabobs, Swiss-Ham, 82
Loaf, Italian Pull-Apart, 145
Prosciutto with Angel Hair, 51
Steak Hawaiian, Ham, 81

Ice Cream
Dream, Ice Cream, 159
Pie, Quick 'n' Easy, 177
Pie, Toffee Ice Cream, 178
Sandwiches, Almond-Ginger Ice
Cream, 160
Shake, PB 'n' Nanner, 27

Lamb Chops, Pecan-Crusted, 47
Lasagna-Chicken Florentine, 58
Lemon
Crispies, Lemon, 184
Green Beans, Lemon-Basil, 100
Honeyade, Lemon, 26
Vermicelli, Lemon, 91

Muffins
Berry Muffins, Merry, 137
Cocktail Muffins, Cheesy, 19
'Nana Muffins, Surprise, 138

Noodle Casserole, Chunky Chicken-, 66
Noodles, Easy Asian Beef and, 70

Okra, and Tomatoes, Corn, 109
Onion Popovers, 139
Oranges
Coffee Cake, Orange-Almond, 152
Sauce, Pork Tenderloin with Orange, 49
Sauce, Shrimp with Jalapeño-Orange, 57

Pastas. *See also* Fettuccine, Lasagna, Noodles.
Angel Hair Pasta, Shrimp Marinara with, 85
Angel Hair, Prosciutto with, 51
Mac 'n' Cheese, Sea Shell, 90
Manicotti with Chive Cream Sauce, Chicken, 41
Penne with Nutty Cream Sauce, Two-Cheese, 60
Salad, Presto Pasta, 130
Tomatoes, Brie, and Basil, Pasta with, 59
Tortellini Soup, Beef-, 120
Vermicelli, Lemon, 91
Peaches
Crisp, Gingered Peach, 182
Pickled Peaches, Spiced, 102
Pork Picante, Peachy, 79
Tea, Peachy, 25
Peanut Butter
Bars, Peanut Butter S'More, 192
Cookies, Easy Peanut Butter, 186
Cups, Peanut Butter, 198
Shake, PB 'n' Nanner, 27
Pear-Walnut Salad, 123
Peas
Black-Eyed Pea Salad, 127
Hoppin' John, Quick, 93
Perfection, Peas to, 101
Sugar Snaps with Sesame Vinaigrette, 104
Pecans
Biscotti, Pecan, 188
Cake, Nutty Graham Picnic, 164
Cheese, Cranberry-Pecan Goat, 13
Lamb Chops, Pecan-Crusted, 47
Praline Chicken, 34
Pralines, Microwave, 199
Peppermint Pie, 179
Peppers
Green Chilie Cornbread, 144
Jalapeño Guacamole, 10
Jalapeño-Orange Sauce, Shrimp with, 57
Pies and Pastries
Black Russian Pie, Frosty, 172
Blueberry Icebox Pie, 171
Cobbler, Almond-Cherry, 181

Pies and Pastries *(continued)*

    Cobbler, Caramel Apple, 170
    Crisp, Gingered Peach, 182
    Ice Cream Pie, Toffee, 178
    Peppermint Pie, 179
    Pepperoni Pie Squares, 21
    Pizzas, Apple Pie, 157
    Puffs, Mighty Marshmallow Crescent, 158
    Quick 'n' Easy Pie, 177
    Skillet Sombrero Pie, 75
    Tartlets, Apricot-Pecan-Brie, 180
    Tomato Pie, 110
    Turnovers, Sausage and Cheese, 80
Pineapple Cream Cake, 165
Pineapple, Marinated, 15
Pizza, Bubble, 72
Pizzas, Apple Pie, 157
Pork. *See also* Ham.
    Chops, Melt-in-Your-Mouth Pork, 78
    Loin, Garlic Lover's Pork, 48
    Medallions with Mustard Sauce, Pork, 50
    Picante, Peachy Pork, 79
    Tenderloin with Orange Sauce, Pork, 49
Potatoes, Rosemary Roasted, 111
Potatoes, Skillet, 112

Quesadillas, Mexi-Cheesy, 87

Raspberry Green Salad, 124
Rice
    Casserole, Mexi Rice 'n' Cheese, 94
    Hoppin' John, Quick, 93
    Risotto in the Microwave, 95
    Timbales, Cumin Rice, 92
    Tomato-Basil Rice, 129

Salad Dressings
    Ranch Dressing, Home-Style, 132
    Sweet 'n' Tangy Salad Dressing, 131
    Tangy-Sweet Dressing, 123
Salads
    Asparagus and Goat Cheese Salad, 125
    Bean and Cilantro Salad, Three-, 126
    Black-Eyed Pea Salad, 127
    Bread, "Salad," 147
    Gelatin Salad, Cranberry-Eggnog, 122
    Green Salad, Raspberry, 124
    Pasta Salad, Presto, 130
    Peaches, Spiced Pickled, 102
    Pear-Walnut Salad, 123

    Rice, Tomato-Basil, 129
    Spinach-Strawberry Salad with Pecans, 128
Salmon Steaks, Savory, 54
Sandwiches
    Cucumber Sandwiches, 16
    Meatball Sandwiches, Mighty, 76
    Roast Beef Sandwiches, Uptown, 77
Sauces
    Artichoke Cream Sauce, Chicken with, 33
    Chive Cream Sauce, Chicken Manicotti with, 41
    Jalapeño-Orange Sauce, Shrimp with, 57
    Mustard Sauce, Pork Medallions with, 50
    Nutty Cream Sauce, Two-Cheese Penne with, 60
    Orange Sauce, Pork Tenderloin with, 49
Sausage and Cheese Turnovers, 80
Scallops, Oven-Roasted, 55
Shrimp
    Baked Shrimp, Louisiana, 86
    Grilled Shrimp, Garlic-Skewered 'n', 56
    Jalapeño-Orange Sauce, Shrimp with, 57
    Marinara with Angel Hair Pasta, Shrimp, 85
Slow Cooker
    Chicky, Slow-and-Easy Asian, 36
Soups. *See also* Chili.
    Beef-Tortellini Soup, 120
    Cantaloupe Soup, Frosty, 114
    Chicken Soup, Mexican, 119
    Corn and Crabmeat Soup, Easy, 118
    Egg Drop Soup, Chinese, 115
    Pimiento Soup, Cream of, 116
    Tomato Soup, Fresh, 117
Spinach
    Florentine, Lasagna-Chicken, 58
    Roll-ups, Popeye's, 17
    Salad with Pecans, Spinach-Strawberry, 128
Squash, Fruited Acorn, 103
Strawberry Salad with Pecans, Spinach-, 128

Tomatoes
    Corn, Okra, and Tomatoes, 109
    Pasta with Tomatoes, Brie, and Basil, 59
    Pie, Tomato, 110
    Rice, Tomato-Basil, 129
    Soup, Fresh Tomato, 117
Tuna Fettuccine, Terrific, 84
Turkey Cutlets, Classy, 69

Veal Parmigiana, 46
Vegetables. *See also* specific types.
    Bread, "Salad," 147
    Chicken Dinner, One-Pot, 67